John Hayden

WORDSWORTH AND THE POETRY OF EPITAPHS

WORDSWORTH AND THE POETRY OF EPITAPHS

D. D. Devlin

BARNES & NOBLE BOOKS
TOTOWA, NEW JERSEY

© D. D. Devlin 1981

All rights reserved. No part of this publication may be
reproduced or transmitted, in any form or by any means,
without permission

First Published in the U.S.A. 1981 by
BARNES & NOBLE BOOKS
81, Adams Drive, Totowa,
New Jersey, 07512
ISBN 0–06–491679–0
LCN 79–55695

Printed in Hong Kong

British Library Cataloguing in Publication Data

Devlin, David Douglas
  Wordsworth and the poetry of epitaphs
  1. Wordsworth, William – Criticism and interpretation
  I. Title
  821'.7   PR5888

ISBN 0–333–21783–7

Contents

Preface

Wordsworth was a polemical critic; his writings on poetry (usually his own poetry), whether the many occasional (but not casual) comments in his letters, or the Preface to *Lyrical Ballads*, or the Preface to the 1815 edition of his poems (with the additional *Essay, Supplementary to the Preface*), are often aggressively defensive and were either designed to forestall possible criticism or were an angry response to the strictures and blindness of his critics. The Preface to *Lyrical Ballads* was written to prepare the way for poems which Wordsworth himself called experimental and because he did not wish to be "censured for not having performed what I never attempted". The *Essay, Supplementary to the Preface* is a rebuke to Jeffrey of the *Edinburgh Review*. To defend himself against all attacks Wordsworth there propounds the myth that the great original writer is never appreciated in his own day; he confidently rejects all that reviewers and "the Public" can say and submits himself instead to the verdict of "the People".

Wordsworth did not place a high value on criticism: "I am not a Critic – and set little value upon the art." In later years (1830) he claimed that he had written the 1800 Preface "at the urgent entreaties of a friend" (Coleridge) and that he regretted having anything to do with it; and in 1845 he was hoping to publish an edition of his poems without "the Prefaces and Supplement".

The *Essays upon Epitaphs* (1810) are quite different; only the first was published in his lifetime and none of them was designed for any special occasion or intended to explain any group of poems or convert an unwilling audience. In these three wise essays (they contain no special pleading, no self-justification, no confused discussion of metrics, no sublimely egotistic view of the

vii

poet, no angry apportioning of blame), as Wordsworth talks of epitaphs a description emerges of his own finest and most typical work and his characteristic mode of "reconcilement of opposites".

List of Abbreviations

EY   Ernest de Selincourt (ed.), *The Letters of William and Dorothy Wordsworth: The Early Years 1787–1805*, 2nd edn, revised C. L. Shaver (Oxford, 1967).

MY   Ernest de Selincourt (ed.), *The Letters of William and Dorothy Wordsworth: The Middle Years 1806–1820*, 2nd edn, revised Mary Moorman and A. G. Hill, 2 vols (Oxford, 1969–70).

LY   Ernest de Selincourt (ed.), *The Letters of William and Dorothy Wordsworth: The Later Years 1821–1850*, 3 vols (Oxford, 1939).

Prose   W. J. B. Owen and Jane Worthington Smyser (eds),
Works   *The Prose Works of William Wordsworth*, 3 vols (Oxford, 1974).

PW   Ernest de Selincourt and Helen Darbishire (eds), *The Poetical Works of William Wordsworth*, 5 vols (Oxford, 1940–9); vols ii and iii revised Helen Darbishire, 2nd edn (Oxford, 1952–4).

1 The Poet in Search of a Public

Well, you see . . . there's pomes and pomes,
and Wudsworth's was not for sich as us.

I

This epigraph reads like an epitaph on Wordsworth's hope that he might be read by ordinary country people, by those very rustics whose language he once considered the most suitable for poetry. The words were spoken some twenty or thirty years after Wordsworth's death by an old man who had at one time been a gardener's boy at Rydal Mount, and they were quoted in a paper read to the Wordsworth Society by H. D. Rawnsley in 1882.[1] They make clear, with great firmness and some regret, Wordsworth's final failure to communicate with a large un-literary public, his failure to be what he insisted a poet must be, a man speaking to men. He never gave up his hopes for such an audience, but as time passed they declined into wistful regret. In a comment dictated to Isabella Fermor in 1843 on his "The Labourers' Noon-day Hymn", Wordsworth said:

> Bishop Ken's 'Morning and Evening Hymns' are, as they deserve to be, familiarly known. Many other hymns have also been written on the same subject; but, not being aware of any designed for Noon-day, I was induced to compose these verses. Often one has occasion to observe Cottage children carrying, in their baskets, dinner to their Fathers engaged in their daily labours in the fields and woods. How gratifying would it be to

me could I be assured that any portion of these stanzas had been sung by such a domestic concert under such circumstances. A friend of mine has told me that she introduced this Hymn into a Village-school which she superintended, and the stanzas in succession furnished her with texts to comment upon in a way which without difficulty was made intelligible to the children, and in which they obviously took delight, and they were taught to sing it to the tune of the old 100th Psalm. (*PW*, iv, p. 428)

But, as Rawnsley's country witnesses make plain, Wordsworth's poetry did not hold children from play, or old men from the chimney corner. For one thing, it was difficult; for another it simply made no concessions to unsophisticated readers. Rawnsley asked an old farmer if he had ever read any of Wordsworth's poems, or had seen any books of his poems in the local farmhouses:

Ay, ay, time or two. But ya're weel aware there's potry and potry. There's potry wi' a li'le bit pleasant in it, and potry sic as a man can laugh at or the childer understand, and some as takes a deal of mastery to make out what's said, and a deal of Wudsworth's was this sort, ye kna. You could tell fra the man's faace his potry would niver have no laugh in it.

His potry was quite different work from li'le Hartley. Hartley 'ud goa running along beside o' the brooks and mak his, and goa in the first oppen door and write what he had got upo' paper. But Wudsworth's potry was real hard stuff, and bided a deal of makking, and he'd keep it in his head for long enough. Eh, but it's queer, mon, different ways folks has of making potry now. Folks goas a deal to see where he's interred; but for my part I'd walk twice distance over Fells to see where Hartley lies. Not but what Mr. Wudsworth didn't stand very high, and was a well-spoken man enough, but quite one to himself.[2]

The farmer makes a distinction between two types of poetry;

there is poetry such as "a man can laugh at or the childer understand", and there is poetry "as takes a deal of mastery to make out what's said". Each kind implies a different audience; the poet can appeal to a simple, large audience or to an educated small one, and the distinction was one which troubled Wordsworth all his life. What kind of an audience was Wordsworth writing for, and what kind of an audience did he wish to have? Rawnsley's rustics not only preferred Hartley Coleridge's poetry to Wordsworth's, they also preferred Hartley as a person. They found Wordsworth's poetry very like the man; they respected him, they found him kindly but did not greatly like him. A former servant at Rydal Mount complained that "he niver asked folk about their work". When he called at a shop he would merely pass the time of day and would go to the other side of the road rather than pass anyone likely to ask too many questions. "He was not a conversable man" and he wasn't companionable. He "never said much to folk, quite different from li'le Hartley, as knawed the insides of cottages for miles round and was welcome at 'em all." By contrast Wordsworth was "distant . . . varra distant", and it seemed to the local people that "he cared nowt about folk". An old cottager's remarks bring us again to the question of Wordsworth and his audience: "He wozn't a man as said a deal to common folk. But he talked a deal to hissen."[3] Yet we know that at least in his earlier years Wordsworth tried to communicate with ordinary men and women of the dales by reading his poems to them, sometimes the most unlikely poems. It is difficult to know what to think when Dorothy Wordsworth says in a letter from Dove Cottage in 1802: "We have our Haircutter below stairs, William is reading the Leech-gatherer to him."[4] (The scene suggests a Beerbohm cartoon.) It is impossible to believe that Wordsworth was communicating anything; there are poems and poems, but such as "The Leech-gatherer" were not for the local haircutter.

All this seems a far cry from the confident statement of the Preface to *Lyrical Ballads* that a poet was a man speaking to men; but, in fact, the confidence was never unqualified. In the Preface, and even earlier, we can see Wordsworth sharply and uneasily

aware of the problem of the poet and his audience (and especially
the problem of Wordsworth and his own audience) and in his
letters and critical writings we can trace through the years
Wordsworth's changing, veering views. Whom did Wordsworth
want to speak to, and to whom did he think he had succeeded in
speaking? What should be the poet's relationship with his
readers? The most interesting thing is that the problem existed at
all, and that Wordsworth could not believe that what had been
true for poets and their readers in the past was any longer true for
himself. It was not a question that had much troubled earlier
poets. Generally, the neo-classic poet had a keen, confident
awareness of his public; he could address either an individual or
his readers in general, but the distinction had little importance.
Goldsmith writes:

> Ye friends to truth, ye statesmen, who survey
> The rich man's joys increase, the poor's decay,
> 'Tis yours to judge how wide the limits stand
> Between a splendid and a happy land.[5]

Pope may speak to and argue with Bathhurst, Bolingbroke or
Arbuthnot, but they are treated as representatives of the
educated, civilised public to whom Goldsmith and Pope speak
responsibly about human affairs. The Renaissance poet is the
public's equal and their spokesman; he shares their values,
assumptions and beliefs and memorably expresses them. He
accurately gauges the responses of his readers and believes with
them in the importance of poetry. The massive congruity
between poet and audience which Johnson could establish in *The
Vanity of Human Wishes* was possible only because he saw that the
poet's task was to offer a traditional human wisdom which would
be acknowledged by every reader. The audience is always a
public audience and never merely a group of friends, or the poet's
family or his devotees. The neo-classic poet could not speak at the
same time to a public audience and a private one. The confusions
in the Epitaph to Gray's *Elegy* show that the public and private
voices are not easily reconciled.

Wordsworth stands at the meeting-point of two views of poetry, of the poet and of the poet's audience. We must see him as in some ways firmly in the Renaissance tradition, as the final great example in English poetry of that tradition, because that was how he saw himself. It was a stance which puzzled his friends and was misinterpreted by his enemies. He was reluctant to sever the connections between the poet and those public responsibilities with which he had to concern himself; and therefore with complete (though sometimes bizarre) consistency he accepted the office of Distributor of Stamps for Westmorland and later the Laureateship. Earlier, in 1809, he had published his attack on the Convention of Cintra and throughout his life he busied himself with such political matters as the liberty of the press, parliamentary reform, Catholic emancipation and education. It was a busyness which disconcerted his friends: Lamb and Coleridge regretted that so great a poet should spend his time on anything other than poetry, and Coleridge saw political concerns interfering with the writing of that promised great work, *The Recluse*. But Wordsworth did not repent or change his ways and, indeed, used to claim with some pride that for every hour spent on poetry he had spent twenty on politics. Wordsworth, however, is also a Romantic poet. Different assumptions and conventions govern Romantic poetry, and the Romantic poet's relationship with his audience is different because less sure and more ambiguous. The Renaissance insisted that poetry should instruct by delighting; Keats distrusted poetry that had a palpable design upon us. The Romantic poet either communes with himself so that "his poetry is not heard, but overheard", or he adopts the role of seer and prophet, and his voice is Blake's "voice of the Bard". But as seer his fate is always to be Cassandra's, and as prophet he is without honour in his own country. In both cases he has given up the search for a public; he has lost contact with every audience except for a few disciples, a small spiritual or moral élite. He is willing to do without even these and beat "in the void his luminous wings in vain". Wordsworth is at this meeting-point of Renaissance and Romantic views of poetry and their different implications for the kind of audience the poet will have or will wish to have.

Wordsworth never gave up the search for an audience but could never be sure that he had found one. His prefaces and critical essays and letters tell the story of his search for a public and for a satisfactory relationship with that public. Is the poet a man among men, speaking to men? Or is he what we find (for perhaps the first time in English literature) in the Epitaph to Gray's *Elegy*, where the certainties of the poem give way to the uncertainties of the poet's role, a man apart, "with an uneasy consciousness of a sensibility and imagination at once unique and burdensome".[6] Wordsworth may sometimes seem to contradict himself, but it is fairer (and much more helpful) to see his comments as a heroic attempt at inclusiveness, an attempt at that "reconciliation of opposites" which was in so many ways his greatest achievement.

2

Before 1798 Wordsworth seems to have given little thought to the question of the poet and his public; his letters contain no discussion of the matter and there is scarcely an awareness that such a problem might ever arise. Why should it? His two long early poems in heroic couplets, "An Evening Walk" and *Descriptive Sketches* (both published in 1793), brought with them no Advertisement or Preface. If, for all the distinction of many single lines, the poems strike us today as unoriginal, as the last (but distinguished) examples of a dying literary tradition, it is partly because the poet assumes a traditional relationship between writer and reader. The poems imply an educated audience capable of catching literary allusions, a cultured public able to enjoy the formal play of yet another variation on a conventional genre, the "loco-descriptive poems" familiar to it in Denham's *Cooper's Hill*, Dyer's *Grongar Hill* or (Wordsworth's favourite) the Countess of Winchilsea's *A Nocturnal Reverie*. Yet in 1787 Dorothy Wordsworth mentions in a letter that she and William had read and admired the Kilmarnock edition of Burns's poems (1786). In the preface to this edition Burns implies a wish for a new (and wider) audience and for a new relationship with it:

The following trifles are not the production of the Poet, who, with all the advantages of learned art, and perhaps amid the elegancies and idlenesses of upper life, looks down for a rural theme, with an eye to Theocrites or Virgil. . . . Unacquainted with the necessary requisites for commencing Poet by rule, he sings the sentiments and manners, he felt and saw in himself and his rustic compeers around him, in his and their native language.[7]

The first sentence could be a description of the Wordsworth who wrote "An Evening Walk". The "elegancies and idlenesses of upper life" is, in its rejection of one kind of poetry and public, close to Wordsworth's later rejection of "the Public"; but Burns's simpler intention to write a different poetry for a different public in a different language was not one (because it rejected comprehensiveness) which Wordsworth was ever willing to copy. Burns, of course, is adopting a stance; but the pretended rejection of Art, the identification of himself with his "rustic compeers" and the assumption that he shares with these compeers a common language, represent only one of the poles between which Wordsworth continually moved:

> I am nae *Poet*, in a sense,
> But just a *Rhymer* like by chance,
> An' hae to Learning nae pretence . . .[8]

But Wordsworth insisted all his life that poetry was an art: "I have used the word *art*, from a conviction, which I am called upon almost daily to express, that poetry is infinitely more of an art than the world is disposed to believe."[9] The more effectively it is art, the more it will succeed in communicating with all men; and "Every great Poet is a Teacher: I wish to be considered as a Teacher, or as nothing."[10] Such a poet cannot view his public in the same easy way as the poet who sings to his rustic compeers about their sentiments and manners.

The poles between which Wordsworth moved, or the contradictions which he strove to resolve, are already present in his earliest published critical comments, the Advertisement to the first edition of *Lyrical Ballads* (1798). Wordsworth is clearly addressing the educated readers of poetry and he makes clear that the poems which follow must be considered as "experiments". He recognises that "Readers accustomed to the gaudiness and inane phraseology of many modern writers will find the poems strange and may even wonder if they deserve to be called poems at all"; but this will be because they are misled by "that most dreadful enemy to our pleasures, our own pre-established codes of decision", in this case too rigid a definition of poetry. Wordsworth then admits to "readers of superior judgment" that they may think he has occasionally "descended too low" and used expressions which are "too familiar, and not of sufficient dignity"; but (strangely) the reader who is really educated, who is thoroughly read in "our elder writers", will have few complaints. Wordsworth seems to be in the unexpected position of offering poems which only a very cultured and literary public will appreciate. Sir Joshua Reynolds (whose *Discourses* on the principles of art are a handbook of neo-classic criticism which Wordsworth never tired of praising) is brought in to reinforce the point that

> An accurate taste in poetry and in all other arts . . . is an acquired talent, which can only be produced by severe thought, and a long continued intercourse with the best models of composition.

But Wordsworth is aiming not simply at the "Readers of superior judgment" or Johnson's "common reader" but at a public which is scarcely accustomed to reading any poetry at all; and so he goes on (in another direction) to explain that he quoted Sir Joshua with approval

> not with so ridiculous a purpose as to prevent the most inexperienced reader from judging for himself; but [another half-turn] merely to temper the rashness of decision, and to suggest that if poetry be a subject on which much time has not

been bestowed, the judgment may be erroneous, and that in many cases it necessarily will be so.[11]

There is some uncertainty here as to which way he should face; but there is also an engaging confidence that there need be no difficulty (given the good-will on which he easily counts) in making the experiments appeal to all sorts and conditions of men.

Peter Bell, which was written in the same year as the Advertisement, gives an attractive picture of the kind of audience Wordsworth wanted and of his ideal relationship with it. The picture, however, is complicated because there are *two* audiences at least, and possibly three. There is the sophisticated audience to whom the Prologue is directed, and yet in it the poet is talking to himself; when he speaks to the "little boat" he is addressing his own imagination. Then there is the audience to whom he tells the tale proper; this is itself a structure of some ironic complexity, for the listeners to the tale cannot understand why he begins to tell it so incoherently; but we, the readers, know that, like Keats at the end of *Ode to a Nightingale* or the Knight at the end of *La Belle Dame Sans Merci*, the poet is not yet

> wholly rescued from the pale
> Of a wild dream, or worse illusion.

Wordsworth is at ease with both audiences. The opening line of the Prologue, "There's something in a flying horse", implies a literary audience quick to catch the casual allusion to Pegasus, and it is assumed some stanzas later that they will know the meaning of "Hippogriff". The poet recognises that he cannot be a pilgrim of the sky; he cannot speak to people from a "sky-canoe", but must "Descend from this ethereal height", come "back to Earth, the dear green Earth" and speak to his audience of "life's daily prospect" in a language all can understand. He is able to say all this with a relaxed, good-humoured, serious whimsy, with a casual, ironic silliness that implies confidence in, and control of his readers.

The audience to whom the poet tells the tale of Peter Bell is specified:

There is a party in the Bower
Round the stone table in my garden
The Squire is there, and as I guess
His pretty little daughter Bess
With Harry the Churchwarden . . .

There sits the Vicar and his Dame;
And there my good friend, Stephen Otter . . .

and the poet knows them all. The size of the audience does not matter, but its composition is important for it includes educated readers, inexperienced readers and children. More impressive still is Wordsworth's relationship with them; they have waited "anxiously and long" for him and are not afraid to interrupt him and complain when he seems to be making a mess of the story:

"My dearest Sir," cried Mistress Swan
"You've got at once into the middle,"
And little Bess in accents sweeter
Cried "O dear Sir, but who is Peter?"
Said Harry "'Tis a downright riddle." (*PW*, ii, pp. 337, 339)

The audience is well-disposed towards the poet, and the narrative confidence flows from this. The listeners do not interrupt again, but Wordsworth confirms and sustains the established intimacy between himself and his representative audience by occasional deft touches. The story proper begins with the words

"One night, (and now, my little Bess!
We've reached at last the promised Tale) . . ."

In the second part of the poem there is a reference to "kind listeners, that around me sit", and throughout the narrative

Wordsworth, as narrator, uses the uncharacteristic pronoun "we". He will never again be so much at ease.

The poems in the 1798 and 1800 editions of *Lyrical Ballads* seldom show Wordsworth uncertain of his public. One exception is "Michael" in the 1800 edition. The sub-title "A Pastoral Poem" implies an audience acquainted with the pastoral conventions, and part of the effect of the poem results from his disappointing the expectations which in a literary audience the word "pastoral" might arouse. But in the poem itself he speaks to several different audiences. In the opening line, "If from the public way you turn your steps", Wordsworth draws the common reader into a formal intimacy and then treats him with courtesy and firm modesty:

> It is in truth an utter solitude;
> Nor should I have made mention of this Dell
> But for one object which you might pass by,
> Might see and notice not.

Wordsworth never entirely loses touch with this public:

> There stood the urchin, as you will divine,
> Something between a hindrance and a help

and though always polite, he can suggest a criticism of the reader:

> And grossly that man errs, who should suppose
> That the green valleys, and the streams and rocks
> Were things indifferent to the Shepherd's thoughts.

Very early in the poem Wordsworth addresses two other groups who will form more sympathetic, though much smaller, audiences:

> Therefore, although it be a history
> Homely and rude, I will relate the same
> For the delight of a few natural hearts;

And, with yet fonder feeling, for the sake
Of youthful Poets, who among the hills
Will be my second self when I am gone. (*PW*, ii, pp. 81, 82)

Wordsworth is here the self-conscious artist who puts his trust in a moral élite ("a few natural hearts") or, with greater confidence, in writers like himself. The poet is here a man speaking to poets. ("Strange fits of passion" is defensively addressed to a very small and special audience; as the opening stanza reminds us, the poet will "dare" to tell the story "But in the Lover's ear alone". Wordsworth was right to be defensive but it did not save the poem from Jeffrey's scorn.)[12] "Michael" is in no way affected by these uncertainties (it is possible to see them as a less successful attempt at comprehensiveness of the kind we saw in *Peter Bell*) but they are a shadow of things to come.

Coleridge insisted that the Preface to *Lyrical Ballads* had increased Wordsworth's difficulties:

> In the critical remarks, therefore, prefixed and annexed to the *Lyrical Ballads*, I believe, we may safely rest, as the true origin of the unexampled opposition which Mr. Wordsworth's writings have been since doomed to encounter. The humbler passages in the poems themselves were dwelt on and cited to justify the rejection of the theory. What in and for themselves would have been either forgotten or forgiven as imperfections, or at least comparative failures, provoked direct hostility when announced as intentional, as the result of choice after full deliberation. Thus the poems, admitted by all as excellent, joined with those which had pleased the far greater number, though they formed two-thirds of the whole work . . . gave wind and fuel to the animosity against both the poems and the poet.[13]

It is true that the second edition (containing the Preface) received a sharper critical reception than the first, and there is something to suggest that it was the second, 1800, volume which gave particular offence. The first edition, indeed, was moderately

successful, and the moderation of the success was accepted
sensibly by Wordsworth and his sister. Dorothy says in a letter
written in September, 1800 that

> My Brother William is going to publish a second edition of the
> Lyrical Ballads with a second volume. . . . The first volume
> sold much better than we expected, and was liked by a much
> greater number of people, not that we had ever much doubt of
> its finally making its way, but we knew that poems so different
> from what have in general become popular immediately after
> their publication were not likely to be admired all at once. The
> first volume I have no doubt has prepared a number of
> purchasers for the second, and independent of that, I think the
> second is much more likely to please the generality of readers.
> (*EY*, pp. 297–8)

Wordsworth's audience is simply "the generality of readers" and
he is prepared to make concessions. The 1798 poems "have not
sold ill", but "it seems that The Ancyent Mariner has upon the
whole been an injury to the volume, I mean the old words and the
strangeness of it have deterred readers from going on".
Wordsworth wishes to leave it out of any second edition and
would "put in its place some little things which would be more
likely to suit the common taste".[14] It is the last time that he will
be willing to stoop to conquer.

The Preface to *Lyrical Ballads* which we usually read is a
composite document. The first and shortest version was published with the two-volume edition of *Lyrical Ballads* in 1800. In
the 1802 and 1805 editions the Preface was much enlarged, and
in 1836 it was modified in several ways. In 1802 Wordsworth
added the "What is a Poet?" passage and the Appendix on
"what is usually called POETIC DICTION". These later changes to
the 1800 Preface are important if we are to follow the flux and
reflux of Wordsworth's thinking about his public, but the 1800
Preface itself continues the contradictions, or tensions, already
present in the 1798 Advertisement. "Low and rustic life was
generally chosen", and the language of men in such a condition

was used because they express themselves in "simple and unelaborated expressions"; they "speak a plainer and more emphatic language" which makes communication with a large public more easy, immediate and satisfactory for the poet. The language of such men, of course, must be "purified from . . . all lasting and rational courses of dislike or disgust", and the poet, therefore, will be able to use only a "selection of the real language" of such men.[15] Coleridge made the obvious point that "a rustic's language, purified from all provincialisms and grossness . . . will not differ from the language of any other men of common sense"; and since the rustic has fewer notions to communicate and "aims almost solely to convey insulated facts",[16] the adoption of such language will inevitably limit the poet's public. Wordsworth knew this; the blurring phrases are an attempt to insist simultaneously that poetry is art and that it must communicate easily and be "well adapted to interest mankind permanently". Elsewhere in the Preface he draws upon Sir Joshua Reynolds and repeats the words he had quoted in the Advertisement, that "an accurate taste in poetry . . . is an acquired talent, which can only be produced by severe thought, and long continued intercourse with the best models", with the implication that the poet's audience will be necessarily small and confined to the leisured and cultured few. It is, Wordsworth concedes, particularly difficult in these times for the "in-experienced reader" to exercise a right judgement of poetry. Instead of blaming the reader (or the poet) Wordsworth blames the spirit of the age: "For a multitude of causes unknown to former times are now acting with a combined force to blunt the discriminating powers of the mind . . . and reduce it to a state of almost savage torpor."[17]

But in the 1800 Preface Wordsworth introduces a notion central to a Romantic theory of poetry which immediately separates the poet from the public and seems to shatter the relationship so firmly assumed and assured in the poetry of previous ages and so attractively sketched in *Peter Bell:*

It is supposed, that by the act of writing in verse an Author makes a formal engagement that he will gratify certain known habits of association, that he not only thus apprizes the Reader that certain classes of ideas and expressions will be found in his book, but that others will be carefully excluded.

Wordsworth goes on to suggest that Shakespeare, Donne, Dryden and Pope all made and kept such a formal agreement. But now things are different:

> I will not take upon me to determine the exact import of the promise which by the act of writing in verse an Author in the present day makes to his Reader; but I am certain it will appear to many persons that I have not fulfilled the terms of an engagement thus voluntarily contracted. (*Prose Works*, i, p. 121)

This is Wordsworth the poet-radical declaring that he reserves the right to *épater le bourgeois*. When Pope shocked or surprised his readers he did so by relying on expectations and then denying them, on a "formal engagement" and then breaking it. Part of the formal agreement was the use of traditional genres, but Wordsworth rejects the very notion of any contract implied in the use of accepted genres, agreed subject-matter, or common language. (The belief that the poet's task is to shatter complacency by refusing all agreement with his readers is at the heart of much Romantic poetry and it makes satire impossible.)

By 1802 the emphasis has shifted further. A sentence inserted in 1802 at the end of the passage just quoted makes it clear that the reader who fails to understand Wordsworth's poems is still not exactly to be blamed; it is simply that he has acquired bad reading habits, or wrong expectations of what poetry should offer, by being too "accustomed to the gaudiness and inane phraseology of many modern writers". But if readers are in some sense corrupted, this must increase the gap between the poet and the majority of his readers and diminish any confidence and comfort he may have had in them. The 1802 preface moves in opposite directions; Wordsworth insists that the poet must be like all men, must speak to all men in the language of all men. (The earlier, 1800, concern with rustics and their language is now largely forgotten.) At the same time Wordsworth has an "exalted notion" of the poet, who, if he is to cleanse our corruption and put on incorruption, will of necessity be a different kind of being, a seer, prophet and bard. This reaction appears in the famous "What is a Poet?" addition:

> What is a poet? To whom does he address himself? And what language is to be expected from him? – He is a man speaking to men; a man, it is true, endowed with more lively sensibility, more enthusiasm and tenderness, who has a greater knowledge of human nature, and a more comprehensive soul, than are supposed to be common among mankind.

The concessive "it is true" reveals a creature different not in degree but in kind from ordinary men. In eloquent phrases which look forward to Shelley's *Defence of Poetry* Wordsworth puts forward mighty claims for the poet and his art:

> Poetry is the breath and finer spirit of all knowledge; it is the impassioned expression which is in the countenance of all Science. Emphatically may it be said of the Poet, as Shakespeare hath said of man, 'that he looks before and after'. He is the rock of defence for human nature; an upholder and preserver, carrying everywhere with him relationship and love. In spite of difference of soil and climate, of language and manners, of laws and customs: in spite of things silently gone out of mind, and things violently destroyed; the Poet binds together by passion and knowledge the vast empire of human society, as it is spread over the whole earth, and over all time. (*Prose Works*, i, p. 141)

The powers which Shakespeare found in man are now much more clearly to be discovered in the poet. In Dr Johnson's *Rasselas* Imlac also is eloquent on the role of the poet and uses phrases which are close to Wordsworth's and Shelley's. The poet "must write as the interpreter of nature, and the legislator of mankind, and consider himself as presiding over the thoughts and manners of future generations; as a being superior to time and place". But Johnson mockingly describes Imlac's language as an "enthusiastic fit", an attempt "to aggrandize" his own profession, and Rasselas cries out, "Enough! Thou has convinced me that no man can ever be a poet." Yet even in his "enthusiastic fit" Imlac could see clearly the implications of such a view of the poet for the poet's audience. The poet must "content himself with the slow progress of his name; contemn [disregard] the applause of his own time, and commit his claims to the justice of posterity".[18] This disregard for immediate communication with ordinary men was something which Wordsworth would not accept, and it was only later that he could take any comfort from the thought that he might find his audience in that useful hold-all "posterity". Wordsworth is caught in a Romantic dilemma; as the poet aggrandises his own function and, in the manner of a prophet, mounts his "chariot of fire", he loses touch with his public and cannot know whom his words are reaching. Imlac's proud belief that the poet is the legislator of mankind becomes the proud, lonely defeat of Shelley's vision of the poets as the "unacknowledged legislators of the world". Wordsworth is more painfully caught in the dilemma than any other poet because, in a different sense of the phrase, "he looks before and after". He looks back to the Renaissance tradition of the poet as a responsible speaker on all human affairs and forward to the romantic and modern view of the poet's voice as at once prophetic and private. He looks back to a poetry which used accepted literary genres and accepted literary styles (Decorum) and forward to a poetry in which the poet's personal private vision dictates the shape and movement of his work. Because Wordsworth looks before and after he has two different kinds of thing to say, two different voices in which to say them and therefore a problem of communication with an uncertain public.

The references so far have been to Wordsworth's published comments on his poems and his public, but his letters for the years 1801–2 reveal his dilemma more sharply. In April 1801 Wordsworth is sure that his poems "had not altogether failed in my attempt to excite tender sensations in the hearts of my Readers". He thanks his correspondent (a minor poet, John Taylor, to whom he had sent the two-volume *Lyrical Ballads* for comment) for saying that he had found in the poems the "pathos of humanity", and Wordsworth adds that "this is the very excellence at which I aimed". He also sent a copy of both volumes in January of the same year to Charles James Fox. In the accompanying letter Wordsworth admits that only several of the poems "are written upon subjects, which are the common property of all poets"; he is sure that Fox will have a poor opinion of many of the poems, not because Wordsworth thinks poorly of them, but because of the different circles in which they have moved. A poet is a man speaking to men, but not necessarily to Fox and his friends. Wordsworth particularly draws Fox's attention to two poems in the collection, "The Brothers" and "Michael". In these he has

> attempted to draw a picture of the domestic affections as I know they exist among a class of men who are now almost confined to the North of England. They are small independent *proprietors* of land . . . who daily labour on their own little properties.

This class of men, Wordsworth laments, is now being destroyed by "the spreading of manufactures through every part of the country . . . by workhouses, Houses of Industry, and the invention of Soup-shops etc. etc.". Fox must be concerned at these economic and social changes and he is therefore invited to read the poems for the sake of the message if not the medium. Fox is a member of that educated, responsible public which the great eighteenth-century poets addressed with such confidence, and Wordsworth speaks to Fox as an equal and as a man who shares Wordsworth's concern:

> You, Sir, have a consciousness upon which every good man will congratulate you, that the whole of your public conduct has in one way or other been directed to the preservation of this

class of men, and those who hold similar situations. You have
felt that the most sacred of all property is the property of the
Poor.

Fox is one of those "friends to truth" and "statesmen" to whom
Goldsmith appeals in *The Deserted Village*. One difference is that
Wordsworth speaks to Fox in a letter and not in the poems
because (as Wordsworth explains in the letter) the main purpose
of the poems is something less public, less overtly didactic: "The
two poems which I have mentioned were written to shew that
men who do not wear fine clothes can feel deeply." Yet
Wordsworth, with the most oblique and tactful of rebukes,
suggests that Fox should be able to see ("whatever effect they [the
two poems] may have upon you") that Wordsworth is still
addressing if not quite all men, at least "many kind and good
hearts" of whom (naturally) Fox is one. The phrase is an
enlargement of the "few natural hearts" whom he mentions in
"Michael" as one of his publics.

In a letter to John Wilson[19] in June 1802 Wordsworth is more
critical of his readers. The tone of the letter is one of uneasy
condescension: "It is plain from your letter that the pleasure
which I have given you has not been blind or unthinking you
have studied the poems . . . They have not given you a cheap or
vulgar pleasure." Condescension is followed by passionate but
polite rebuke for a mildly recalcitrant devotee. (John Wilson is
perhaps the first member of the reading public to be rebuked for
not understanding what the master was about.) Wilson had not
much liked "The Idiot Boy"; it was not, he thought, a proper
subject for poetry and he generalised his objection: "There are a
thousand occurrences happening every day which do not in the
least interest an unconcerned spectator." Wordsworth's answer
takes him at once to the question of the poet's public: "You begin
what you say upon the Idiot Boy with this observation, that
nothing is a fit subject for poetry which does not please. But here
follows a question, Does not please whom?" The answer is
"human nature, as it has been and ever will be". Human nature
can best be discovered in "men who lead the simplest lives most

according to nature"; that is, in men "who have never known false refinements, wayward and artificial desires, false criticisms, effeminate habits of thinking and feeling, or who, having known these things, have outgrown them". The sudden alternative offered at the end of this sentence is important because "This latter class is the most to be depended upon, but it is very small in number." Human nature can be found among the educated and cultured, but only when they have acquired a new innocence. A poet's success is not to be measured by the size of his audience. If he reaches only a few, these few will be the only fit representatives of human nature. The poet is a teacher ("Every great Poet is a Teacher. I wish to be considered as a Teacher, or as nothing") and must educate his readers, must rectify their feelings and "render their feelings more sane, pure and permanent". The notion of teacher is here much extended. "Each of my poems has a purpose", Wordsworth had said in the Preface, but some years later he makes clear in the *Letter to a Friend of Burns* (1816) how he was glossing these words. Wordsworth describes some of the scenes in *Tam O' Shanter* and says, "I pity him who cannot perceive that, in all this, though there was no moral purpose, there is moral effect".[20] This "moral effect" seems to be that "intelligent sympathy", mentioned by Wordsworth a few lines later, which is kindled in the reader by the sympathetic imagination of the poet.

Wordsworth is moving steadily to a position where he believes that only a "few natural hearts" can read his poetry, can be worthy disciples. Only the pure of heart will be able to see "into the spirit" of what he writes; but as time passed it became clear to him that only the pure in heart wanted to. His anger with the hard hearts and blindness of men increased as he found his fit audience becoming fewer, and sometimes not fit enough. The consciousness of a small and shrinking audience explains the ferocity of his reactions when any one of the few seemed to be questioning their mentor. He has already moved away from that earlier willingness to add to the second edition of *Lyrical Ballads* "some little things which would be more likely to suit the common taste". Sara Hutchinson, and even Mary, are rebuked for not liking "the latter part of the Leech-gatherer". Wordsworth gives them a prose summary of the earlier stanzas leading to the appearance of the old man:

'Now whether it was by peculiar grace, A leading from above'. A person reading this Poem with feelings like mine will have been awed and controuled, expecting almost something spiritual or supernatural . . . You say and Mary (that is you can say no more than that) the Poem is *very well* after the introduction of the old man; this is not true, if it is not more than very well it is very bad, there is no intermediate state. You speak of his speech as tedious: everything is tedious when one does not read with the feelings of the Author – '*The Thorn*' is tedious to hundreds; and so is the *Idiot Boy* to hundreds. It is in the character of the old man to tell his story in a manner which an impatient reader must necessarily feel as tedious.

Dorothy in the same letter cautions Sara:

When you happen to be displeased with what you suppose to be the tendency or moral of any poem which William writes, ask yourself whether you have hit upon the real tendency and true moral . . . and when you feel any poem of his to be tedious, ask yourself in what spirit it was written . . . (*EY*, pp. 366–7)

The reader must read "with the feelings of the author". Does this mean that the poet can reach only the converted? Certainly Wordsworth is moving towards an argument which he will develop later, that the goodness of a poem will depend in part on the moral and imaginative fitness of the reader.

3

Wordsworth's *Poems in Two Volumes* (1807) was badly received; only one of the thirteen reviews in magazines was favourable.[21] One immediate result was that Wordsworth decided to postpone publication of *The White Doe of Rylstone*; a more important result was a hardening attitude towards the public and a hardening conviction of his own rightness. His letters for the years 1807 and 1808 make clear the changes in his critical position and also his continued yearning for a more relaxed relationship with a larger audience. Even Jeffrey in his dismissive review seemed to remind Wordsworth that he could have kept a larger public: "The Lyrical Ballads were unquestionably popular, and, we have no hesitation in saying, deservedly popular . . ." Lady Beaumont wrote to express dismay and disappointment at the critical reception of the poems. In his answer Wordsworth claims that he foresaw how his poems would be received, and he moves towards a distinction between "you and my other Friends" and the great uncomprehending Public (it is given a capital letter) which is identified as the enemy and showered with contempt.[22] By its very nature, by its daily concern with worldly things, the Public cannot ever appreciate his poetry:

> The things which I have taken, whether from within or without, – what have they to do with routs, dinners, morning calls, hurry from door to door, from street to street, on foot or in Carriage; with Mr. Pitt or Mr. Fox . . . the Westminster Election or the Borough of Honiton . . .

Mr Fox, who had earlier been assumed by Wordsworth to be a natural member of that educated public which he had once taken as at least a possible audience for his poetry, has gone over to the enemy; he is now one of the Public, one of these people who "in the senseless hurry of their idle lives do not *read* books", but merely "snatch a glance at them". The vanity and selfishness of the Public come between it and Wordsworth's poems. And this dread Public is very large indeed: "It is an awful truth, that there neither is, nor can be, any genuine enjoyment of Poetry among nineteen out of twenty of those persons who live, or wish to live, in the broad light of the world." (The fraction "nineteen out of twenty" sounds like a polite escape clause for Lady Beaumont, for she and her husband certainly lived in the world's broad light.) "And this truth is an awful one," Wordsworth continues, "because to be incapable of a feeling of Poetry in my sense of the word is to be without love of human nature and reverence for God." The language makes it unambiguously clear that Wordsworth equates an ability to read his poetry with a form of salvation; it is a poetry, indeed, for all men, but only the Elect can receive it.

But Wordsworth could never accept that he was speaking only to a few, so in the same letter he discovers a new, vast audience with whom he will easily communicate in the years ahead, a flock whom he, the shepherd, will gently lead. "Trouble not yourself", he says to Lady Beaumont with a Biblical echo:

> Trouble not yourself upon their present reception; of what moment is that compared with what I trust is their destiny, to console the afflicted, to add sunshine to daylight by making the happy happier, to teach the young and the gracious of every age, to see, to think and feel, and therefore to become more actively and securely virtuous; this is their office, which I trust they will faithfully perform long after we (that is, all that is mortal of us) are mouldered in our graves.

How very few can enter the kingdom of heaven which is Wordsworth's *Poems in Two Volumes*! In outer darkness are not simply "London wits and witlings" but "respectable persons" and "grave kindly-natured persons, who would be pleased if they could". Wordsworth hopes that some of his poems will have appeal "even for Readers of this class", but at the same time knows that they cannot, "for their imagination has slept" and the trumpet of his poetry is not able to wake them. The new great host whom Wordsworth's trumpet *will* awaken is Posterity; but certainty of posterity's approval does not conceal the pessimistic present position. He interrupts his explanatory comments to Lady Beaumont with the words, "But I am wasting words, for it is nothing more than you know, and if I said it to those for whom it is intended, it would not be understood." A proper judge of the poetry already knows it is good; that is what makes him a proper judge.

If Wordsworth remains unread or misunderstood it is not simply because of an alien Public. In the same letter he introduces a new principle to explain the great gulf fixed between himself and the majority of readers; he insists that no great poet can ever be appreciated by his contemporaries:

> never forget what I believe was observed to you by Coleridge, that every great and original writer, in proportion as he is great or original, must himself create the taste by which he is to be relished; he must teach the art by which he is to be seen; this, in a certain degree, even to all persons, however wise and pure may be their lives, and however unvitiated their taste; but for those who dip into books in order to give an opinion of them, or talk about them to take up an opinion – for this multitude of unhappy, and misguided, and misguiding beings, an entire regeneration must be produced; and if this be possible, it must be a work *of time*.

This is comprehensive; there is not, after all, even one reader in twenty – not even, it seems, Lady Beaumont – who can truly relish Mr Wordsworth's good wine. The change in taste will also be a moral change; the word "regeneration" makes clear that only the good man can hope to be the good reader. It is also contradictory since it makes it possible for the "wits and witlings" eventually to see the light. The effect will be that of co-operative Grace; he has an "invincible confidence" that his poetry "will co-operate with the benign tendencies in human nature and society, wherever found". There is no contradiction between Wordsworth's "calm confidence that these Poems will live" and his angry vexation at their reception. Posterity was indeed an audience which could not answer back, but it was always his last refuge. Wordsworth never wanted to be a minority poet; he could not renounce the traditional public role of the poet as a man speaking to men and not simply to men as yet unborn. His own poetry relied on and required an immediate reader whom

Wordsworth could draw into intimacy, a reader whom
Wordsworth might either formally address, or confide in, or
make fun of in a Fielding-like fashion in order to secure witty or
dramatic effects. In "Simon Lee" Wordsworth beguiles the
reader into following a story which exactly illustrates the
argument in the Preface that in the poems in *Lyrical Ballads* "the
feeling therein developed should give importance to the action
and situation, and not the action and situation to the feeling".
Half-way through the poem Wordsworth suddenly turns to the
reader:

> My gentle Reader, I perceive
> How patiently you've waited
> And now I fear that you expect
> Some tale will be related
>
> O Reader! had you in your mind
> Such stores as silent thought can bring,
> O gentle Reader! you would find
> A tale in every thing.
> What more I have to say is short,
> And you must kindly take it:
> It is no tale; but, should you think,
> Perhaps a tale you'll make it.(*PW*, iv, p. 63)

The tone is a marvellous mixture, such as we can find in Fielding,
of polite rebuke, gentle mockery and seriousness. The writer
knows with confidence what his readers' reactions will be; he
relies on those reactions and can therefore ironically disappoint
them; but the disappointment is the means to new insights. In all
this we have the confidence of a writer, not the faith of a prophet.
No writing can be more relaxed and intimate than this, none
more immediately directed to the reader here and now, none less
concerned with the distant ear and approval of posterity.[23]

In a letter to Sir George Beaumont in February of the
following year, 1808, Wordsworth continues his attack on the
Public and his search for readers. He warns Sir George (who had

prepared a picture for *Peter Bell*) that "no poem of mine will ever
be popular", but seems to mean immediately popular on
publication; he is not doubting the response of future readers. He
brusquely suggests that a poet should "first consult his own heart
as I have done and leave the rest to posterity; to, I hope, an
improving posterity". Wordsworth had already delayed the
publication of *Peter Bell* for ten years and would wait for another
nine. He had enough experience of reviewers and of the Public
with its "sickly taste" to know that the poem would scarcely
please them; but he makes a new, sharp and important
distinction: "The *People* would love the poem of Peter Bell, but
the Public (a very different Being) will never love it."[24]
Wordsworth will have more to say about this distinction some
years later. "The *People*" suggests Wordsworth's yearning to
communicate widely, and his belief that somewhere, and not
simply in posterity, there was an audience whom it might be
possible for him to reach. But in the meantime it is not at all clear
what readers or what men make up the People. It cannot be the
poet's family and friends and there has been no mention for some
time of those in "humble and rustic life" who might be reached in
poems whose language closely matched their own simple expression. Two months later, however, Wordsworth seems to have
met one of the People on a coach journey, as he mentions in
another letter to Sir George Beaumont:

> At Lancaster I happened to mention Grasmere in hearing of
> one of the Passengers, who asked me immediately if one
> Wordsworth did not live there. I answered, 'Yes'. 'He has
> written', he said, 'some very beautiful Poems; The Critics do
> indeed cry out against them, and condemn them as *over simple*,
> but for my part I read them with great pleasure, they are
> natural and true.' – This man was also a Grocer. (*MY*, i, p. 210)

If the grocer had not existed it would have been necessary to
invent him.

By the summer of 1808 the discomfort of Wordsworth's
position is clear from other letters. In the month of May Dorothy

writes to a friend that Wordsworth would be willing to publish
The White Doe of Rylstone "for the sake of the money" but cannot
see that it would earn him anything. "He has no pleasure in
publishing – he even detests it – and if it were not that he is *not*
over wealthy, he would leave all his works to be published after
his Death."[25] The gloom of this extreme position passes, and in a
letter written to Francis Wrangham in June Wordsworth's old
wish that he might find readers wistfully reasserts itself. He
admits that "as far as my own observation goes, which has been
mostly employed upon agricultural Persons in thinly-peopled
districts, I cannot find that there is much disposition to read
among the labouring classes, or much occasion for it". He goes on
to talk of the "half-penny Ballads, and penny and twopenny
histories" which are hawked about the cottages and adds that

> I have many a time wished that I had talents to produce songs,
> poems, and little histories, that might circulate among other
> good things in this way, supplanting partly the bad; flowers
> and useful herbs to take place of weeds. Indeed some of the
> Poems which I have published were composed not without a
> hope that at some time or other they might answer this purpose.
> (*MY*, i, p. 248)

The wish is a poignant confession of failure. F. W. Bateson has
commented on the absence of folk-lore and folk-song in
Wordsworth's poetry, and his letters and the comments of those
who knew him confirm his almost total ignorance of these things.
It is unlikely, therefore, that the people whom he met in his daily
walks, the beggars and old soldiers and leech-gatherers, could
ever have become "the *People*" of his vision.

Other letters of the period show his retreat from earlier hopes.
He commiserates with Scott in case *Marmion* should be less well
received than *The Lay of the Last Minstrel*; "had the Poem been
much better than the Lay – it could scarcely have satisfied the
Public, which at best has too much of the monster, the moral
monster, in its composition".[26] He need not have worried. In
spite of Jeffrey's unfavourable comments *Marmion* was more

popular than *The Lay*, and this popularity with the despised
Public later annoyed Wordsworth. By 1833 he refuses to allow
that Scott and Byron are popular writers at all, probably because
the word suggests Wordsworth's cherished People; instead,
"perhaps the word ought rather to be that they are *fashionable*
writers",[27] fit reading, no doubt, for the Public and the wits and
witlings. In September 1808 Wordsworth began to concern
himself with the reform of the laws concerning authors' copyright. In that year it was proposed to extend the right from
fourteen years after the death of a writer to twenty-eight, but

> this I think far too short a period; at least I am sure that it
> requires much more than that length of time to establish the
> reputation of original productions, both in Philosophy and
> Poetry, and to bring them consequently into such circulation
> that the authors in the Persons of their Heirs or posterity, can in
> any degree be benefited, I mean in a pecuniary point of view,
> for the trouble they must have taken to produce the works.
> (*MY*, i, p. 266)

He is anxious for a further extension because he is increasingly
certain that only posterity will be just to him or to any great and
original talent. The existing laws of copyright favour "flimsy and
shallow writers, whose works are upon a level with the taste and
knowledge of the age", but are unjust to "men of real power who
go before their age"; and therefore "what matters it who is
pleased or displeased".

4

The search for a public may not be Wordsworth's first concern in
his *Essays upon Epitaphs* (1810), but much of their interest comes
from the implications of what he says for his own poetic practice
and for the relationship of the poet to his readers. Wordsworth
has moved away from dismay and anger at his own reception by
the public, from the scolding and contempt of the letters and from
the theoretical self-justification of the Preface. The *Essays* are not

polemical; his first concern is no longer a search for readers. He
tells us that the subject of epitaphs had occupied his mind for ten
years and that it was the reading of Chiabrera's epitaphs which
finally moved him to write. All three essays were written early in
1810. The first essay was published in Coleridge's *The Friend* on
22 February 1810 but the remaining two remained unpublished
until 1876.

In these essays Wordsworth finds that the writer's sweetest
hope of speaking to many and being heard by many lies in the
epitaph. Words engraven on a stone may be read with especial
poignancy by a small group of the dead man's friends, but they
are addressed to every passer-by, they speak to all men and they
will reach and instruct posterity. An epitaph is a "reconcilement", is both a private and a public writing; it is not simply "for
a satisfaction to the sorrowing hearts of the survivors" but for
"the common benefit of the living". It was the custom among the
Greeks and Romans to bury their dead by the way sides, and
Wordsworth considers the advantages of these lonely epitaphs in
country places:

> Many tender similitudes must these objects [trees, flowers,
> streams] have presented to the mind of the traveller leaning
> upon one of the tombs, or reposing in the coolness of its shade,
> whether he had halted from weariness or in compliance with
> the invitation, 'Pause, Traveller!' so often found upon the
> monuments. And to its epitaph also must have been supplied
> strong appeals to visible appearances or immediate im-
> pressions, lively and affecting analogies of life as a journey –
> death as a sleep overcoming the tired wayfarer – of misfortune
> as a storm that falls suddenly upon him. . . . These, and similar
> suggestions, must have given, formerly, to the language of the
> senseless stone a voice enforced and endeared by the benignity
> of that nature with which it was in vision. (*Prose Works*, ii, p. 54)

"Pause, Traveller!" The reader of an epitaph is the audience
Wordsworth wanted: Everyman. Such an epitaph is read by
every passer-by, yet is removed from the busy world; it records a

private event, a private sorrow, yet one which all men have known or will know. "It is concerning all and for all"; and because it is for all men it will make concessions: the writer of an epitaph must stoop to conquer:

> But an epitaph is not a proud writing shut up for the studious: it is exposed to all – to the wise and the most ignorant; it is condescending, perspicuous, and lovingly solicits regard; its story and admonitions are brief, that the thoughtless, the busy, and indolent, may not be deterred, nor the impatient tired: the stooping old man cons the engraven record like a second hornbook; – the child is proud that he can read it; and the stranger is introduced through its mediation to the company of a friend . . . (*Prose Works*, ii, p. 59)

The final phrase seems to hint that the audience for an epitaph extends even beyond posterity and (especially if the epitaph is imagined to be written by the dead person and is placed in a country churchyard) includes the whole communion of the living and the dead.

Since an epitaph is "concerning all and for all" Wordsworth is able to drop finally all reference to low and rustic life as the subject of his verse, and he does not continue the confused argument on the need to express his subject in the language (or even a selection of it) to be found in such low and rustic life. The aim of a funeral monument has from the very earliest times been to preserve the memory of the dead and "as soon as nations learned the use of letters, epitaphs were inscribed upon these monuments; in order that their intention might be more surely and adequately fulfilled". Man's wish to live in the memory of his fellows comes directly from the "consciousness of a principle of immortality in the human soul". The language through which his memory is to live must accordingly be simple, timeless, almost, as we shall see, no language at all. Two lines from one of Pope's epitaphs are dismissed because their "trifling epigrammatic point" makes it difficult to communicate "the beauty and majesty of Truth".

But if neutral language is fittest for an epitaph, then as the language does less the reader must do more, and Wordsworth √ approaches the position that a good reader makes the good poem. (By 1815 the pathetic and the sublime in poetry can achieve nothing "without the exertion of a co-operating *power* in the mind of the Reader".) In the *Essays upon Epitaphs* the expressions are less abstract, perhaps more tentative, but they still suggest that the force of an epitaph (the poetry of an epitaph) is not in the words but in what the reader brings to the words. Not every reader, however, will be able to bring what is needed. An epitaph which might be "wholly uninteresting from the uniformity of the language" will be "thoroughly felt" by the reader who has "previously participated" the epitaph's vital truth. Even the epitaph, Wordsworth begins to suggest (and there are echoes here of what he said in the letters of 1807 and 1808) cannot reach everyone; no reader is fit or able to read an epitaph who does not bring to it co-operating power. "An experienced and well-regulated mind will not, therefore, be insensible to this mono-tonous language of sorrow and affectionate admiration; but will find under that veil a substance of individual truth." Truth can reach the reader in spite of the words; and now it is not only the reader with the well-regulated mind:

> Yet, upon all Men, and upon such a mind in particular, an Epitaph must strike with a gleam of pleasure, when the expression is of that kind which carries conviction to the heart at once that the Author was a sincere mourner, and that the Inhabitant of the Grave deserved to be so lamented. (*Prose Works*, ii, p. 66)

A good epitaph, then, is judged by its "sincerity", an idea to √ which I shall return in the next chapter. In the meantime Wordsworth is less interested in theories of language than in a theory of poetry which requires the co-operation of writer and reader. He is talking at once of epitaphs and poetry (especially his own poetry) when he claims, in a phrase which recalls the preface to *Lyrical Ballads*, that the subject of both is

those primary sensations of the human heart, which are the
vital springs of sublime and pathetic composition, in this and
in every other kind. And, as from these primary sensations such
composition speaks, so, unless correspondent ones listen
promptly and submissively in the inner cell of the mind to
whom it is addressed, the voice cannot be heard: its highest
powers are wasted. (*Prose Works*, ii, p. 70)

The "inward simplicity" of an epitaph (Wordsworth sharply
distinguishes this from simplicity of language: the two need not be
found   together)   cannot   be   tested   "without   habits   of
reflection . . . . and, as I have said, I am now writing with a
hope to assist the well-disposed to attain it". The primary
sensations, if they "be not stifled in the heart of the Reader",
together with "habits of reflection", can turn dross into gold
without the alchemy of art. Without them "neither these nor
more exalted strains can by [the reader] be truly interpreted";
without them the following simple epitaph cannot be "read with
pleasure":

Aged 3 Month
What Christ said once he said to all:
Come unto me, ye Children small;
None shall do you any wrong,
For to my kingdom you belong. (*Prose Works*, ii, p. 92)

The words of this epitaph are simple and few; but no words at all
are better than even a few, and an epitaph or poem which lays all
the burden on the reader has, potentially, all mankind for an
audience. The "silent poet" (the phrase is Wordsworth's)[28] will
speak to all men since, though we do not possess a common
language, we can share a common silence, for "we have all of us
one human heart":

In an obscure corner of a Country Church-yard I once espied,
half-overgrown with Hemlock and Nettles, a very small Stone

laid upon the ground, bearing nothing more than the date of birth and death, importing that it was an Infant which had been born one day and died the following. I know not how far the Reader may be in sympathy with me, but more awful thoughts of rights conferred, of hopes awakened, of remembrances stealing away or vanishing were imparted to my mind by that Inscription there before my eyes than by any other it has ever been my lot to meet with upon a Tomb-stone. (*Prose Works*, ii, p. 93)

5

In March 1815 Wordsworth published *Poems, Including Lyrical Ballads* in two volumes. This was a collected edition of all his earlier shorter poems and of all the short poems written since the 1807 collection. The volumes were provided with a Preface to explain the new arrangement of the poems and an *Essay, Supplementary to the Preface*. At almost the same time *The White Doe of Rylstone* made its long-delayed appearance as a slim quarto; it cost a guinea and the high price slowed its sale. Wordsworth said that he published the poem in quarto "to show the world my opinion of it" but did not expect the world to share his opinion; he simply hoped that it would be "acceptable to the intelligent, for whom it is written". It is not clear whether "the intelligent" are to be found among the Public, or the People, or among his friends or whether it is another word for posterity. The high price (even Coleridge was shocked) is simply a further sign of Wordsworth's proud withdrawal from the struggle to reach any wider reading public. Dorothy, too, regretted the price but knew how her brother was thinking:

It is a pity it was published in so expensive a form because some are thereby deprived of the pleasure of reading it; but however cheap his poems might be I am sure it will be very long before they have an extensive sale – nay it will not be while he is alive to know it. God be thanked he has no *mortification* on this head . . . . His writings will live – will comfort the afflicted

and animate the happy to purer happiness when we and our
little cares are all forgotten. (*MY*, ii, p. 247)

The refuge of the "silent poet" is not available in the polemical
Essay, Supplementary to the Preface (1815). This is Wordsworth's last
formal critical writing (only the short "Letter to a Friend of
Robert Burns" is later) and it takes him further from a neo-classic
to a Romantic view of poetry, the poet and the poet's audience.
Hints and suggestions from the previous fifteen years are given
shape, authority and substance, and in it the poet is revealed, but
still with qualifications, as the purveyor of minority culture. It is
"inevitable" that most men "will for the most part be rather
repelled than attracted by an original Work"; many disqualify
themselves by passing their time away "in a course of fashionable
pleasure" and so come to treat poetry as "a species of luxurious
amusement". "Serious persons" read poetry for the wrong
reasons, "as a consolation for their afflictions", and the young, for
whom "Poetry is, like love, a passion", can escape delusion in
nothing and "are especially subject to it in their intercourse with
poetry". There remain those who, having loved poetry in their
youth, find time in later years to treat poetry "*as a study*" and
bring to it "the last power of their understandings". In this class
only is it possible to find the good critic (that is, reader) of poetry,
for only here can we find "a natural sensibility that has been
tutored into correctness without losing anything of its quickness".
It is possible to find one here but the odds are against it; for if "this
Class comprehends the only judgments which are trustworthy, so
does it include the most erroneous and perverse". These readers
may, indeed, have been tutored into correctness, but "to be
mistaught is worse than to be untaught"; their natural sensibility
may enable them "to be pleased with what is good", but they will
be pleased "only by imperfect glimpses, and upon false principles". If they should ever "generalise rightly, to a certain point,
they are sure to suffer for it in the end"; and if they
should ever "stumble upon a sound rule, are fettered by
misapplying it". Many of these critics, in any case, are found "too
petulant to be passive to a genuine poet, and too feeble to grapple

with him"; they are too slow to follow the poet "if he turn quick upon the wing". They are men of "palsied imaginations and indurated hearts; in whose minds all healthy action is languid". These men, after all, "feed as the many direct them"; they are "judges, whose censure is auspicious, and whose praise ominous"!

We must remember that these "ungracious" remarks (the adjective is Wordsworth's) are applied to the only class of readers whom Wordsworth finds even theoretically qualified to pass trustworthy judgements on his poetry. His dilemma is clear; the readers he has in mind are exactly those who in happier times have formed a poet's audience. They are the educated readers to whom Spenser, Milton, Pope and Johnson had addressed themselves and on whom they had been able to depend. These were the readers Wordsworth wanted (some of them were his friends) and they had failed him. He felt that they had especially failed him only a few months earlier on the publication of *The Excursion* in the summer of 1814. Its critical reception was not unfavourable. Jeffrey, it is true, had memorably announced in the *Edinburgh Review* that "This will never do!" He had found evidence in the poem that "The case of Mr. Wordsworth . . . is now manifestly hopeless", but was willing to "wait in patience for the natural termination of the disorder". But then Wordsworth had expected nothing from Jeffrey; he was simply one of those critics "too petulant to be passive to a genuine poet, and too feeble to grapple with him", and he did not intend to read the review or, as he put it, "pollute my fingers with touching his book". The hurt came from other members of this class who (Wordsworth knew) could be "pleased with what is good", but who on this occasion were not pleased enough. Hazlitt, Lamb and James Montgomery (the hymn writer) all reviewed *The Excursion* and Coleridge commented on it to Lady Beaumont in a letter which she incautiously showed to Wordsworth. All of them found much to praise in the poem (even Jeffrey admitted that the "simple story" of Margaret in Book I was told with "very considerable pathos") and, except for Coleridge, praised it in terms which they must have thought would have pleased the poet. But it was not enough; their praise was qualified. Hazlitt noted that "an intense intellectual egoism swallows up everything"; Montgomery was uneasy with the poem's natural theology; Lamb's high praise was obscured by the mangled form in which his review eventually appeared in the *Quarterly Review*; Coleridge considered it inferior to *The Prelude* (as yet, of course, unpublished). These were critics whom Wordsworth could not despise; and so in the *Essay* of 1815 he turns on them. He admits their love of poetry and allows them natural sensibility; but they are morally and imaginatively blighted creatures ("palsied imaginations") and like fallen men can see only by imperfect glimpses. And in the end Wordsworth comes to the inevitably proud, absurd paradox of the poet as outsider; these critics are "judges whose censure is auspicious, and whose praise ominous". Wordsworth in future will know that he has written well if this class of reader declares that he has written badly. The distance Wordsworth has travelled is clear from some words in Jeffrey's review. Jeffrey thought he would have been a better poet if he had stopped "confining himself almost entirely to the society of the dalesmen and cottagers, and little children, who form the subjects of his book" and had condescended "to mingle a little more with the people that were to read and judge of it". Wordsworth ought to have "mixed familiarly with men of literature and ordinary judgement in poetry"; he should have addressed the common reader. Wordsworth's answer, as we have seen, was that men of literature and ordinary judgement were now corrupted and blind. Their blindness had resulted (as he said in the Preface to *Lyrical Ballads*) from "a multitude of causes, unknown to former times" which were now "acting with a combined force to blunt the discriminating powers of the mind" and which stopped men from seeing new truths more easily visible to those in a less corrupted state, to dalesmen, cottagers and little children.

It seems, however, that in spite of this "multitude of causes" things were never really any better, and in the *Essay, Supplementary to the Preface* Wordsworth clears himself of any blame for the bad reception of *The Excursion* by inventing the most lasting and cherished of Romantic myths, that the great and original poet has never been popular in his own day. Wordsworth needed to create the myth since he did not wish to be considered different from the great poets of the past and was still neo-classic enough in opinion and temperament to shun what Dr Johnson calls "the pride of singularity". Singularity is the "violation of established practice" and it "implies in its own nature a rejection of the common opinion, a defiance of common censure, and an appeal from general laws to private judgment".[29] Wordsworth could evade part of the charge by insisting that what people took for his private judgement was, in fact, his revelation of previously unobserved general laws; or, in Coleridge's phrases, that Wordsworth indeed offered the reader "faithful adherence to the truth of nature" but gave this truth "the interest of novelty by the modifying colours of imagination".[30] But a better way was to claim that he was no more willingly listened to than earlier great poets and that the number of "judges who can be confidently relied upon" is in any age very small. Once again, by putting his public (and the publics of earlier times) in the wrong, he puts himself (and earlier poets) in the right. A corollary to this argument is that minor writers often blaze into sudden popularity and die away as rapidly, and that excessive popularity may hinder the recognition of original talent.

To prove all this Wordsworth gives the reader "a hasty retrospect of the poetical literature of the country for the greater part of the last two centuries"[31] to see if the facts support him. They don't, of course, and as literary history the retrospect is absurd. What is important is Wordsworth's need to create the myth, his need to make common cause with his predecessors by burdening them with a problem of communication which they did not have and with an isolation from the public which was his alone. "Who is there that now reads the 'Creation' of Dubartas? Yet all Europe once resounded with his praise." We can take this as an oblique comment and prophecy on the popularity and probable fate of Scott and Byron, with Spenser, whose *Faerie Queene* "faded" before *The Creation*, as a sixteenth-century Wordsworth. A thesis which tries to establish the unpopularity of

great writers in their own day will have a problem with
Shakespeare. Since the audience for plays is more immediate
than the readers of poetry, playwrights can, perhaps, be excused
from too unbending an attitude; "A dramatic Author, if he write
for the stage, must adapt himself to the taste of the audience, or
they will not endure him; accordingly the mighty genius of
Shakespeare was listened to," and Wordsworth admits that "the
people were delighted". But this admission does not damage the
thesis since Wordsworth, though "not sufficiently versed in stage
antiquities", thinks it likely that the people were equally
delighted with the plays of very inferior contemporary writers,
and that if there had been "a formal contest for superiority
among dramatic writers" Shakespeare might not always have
come first. "At all events, that Shakespeare stooped to accommodate himself to the People, is sufficiently apparent."
Wordsworth's nervousness about the possibility of having to
stoop in this way (although fifteen years earlier he had been
willing to accommodate himself a little in the second edition of
Lyrical Ballads) is clear when he immediately goes on to clear
Shakespeare from the suspicion of stooping too low by insisting,
as "a fact which in my own mind I have no doubt of", that some
of the grossest passages and scenes in his work "were foisted in by
the Players, for the gratification of the many". Later in the *Essay*
Wordsworth makes a desperate effort to extricate himself from his
own contradictions by talking of Shakespeare's "rights as a poet,
contradistinguished from those which he is universally allowed to
possess as a dramatist". The plays were popular but the poetry
wasn't and could not have been, since

> Grand thoughts (and Shakespeare must often have sighed over
> this truth), as they are most naturally and most fitly conceived
> in solitude, so can they not be brought forth in the midst of
> plaudits, without some violation of their sanctity. (*Prose Works*,
> iii, p. 83)

Men create Shakespeare in their own image; here Wordsworth
turns him into an early Romantic poet, proudly unable to

communicate (even Bacon never mentions him) and for long kept alive only by his "dramatic excellence". Somehow or other it must be established that only an élite was able to enjoy Shakespeare for the right reasons and to the right degree; and yet Shakespeare's audience must have been of the varied kind which Wordsworth had wished for and invoked when in 1798 he wrote *Peter Bell.*

Having solved the problem of Shakespeare, Wordsworth has an easier time with Milton, and especially *Paradise Lost.* It is true that 1300 copies of the poem were sold in two years, but this does not prove that they were read. Milton's religious and political opinions "had procured him numerous friends; who, as all personal danger was passed away at the time of publication", would now wish to own a copy of his "master-work", and so Wordsworth can reach the happy conclusion that "few I fear would be left who sought for it on account of its poetical merits".

The immediate success of Pope and Thomson in their own day is more difficult to explain and must therefore be explained away. Pope aimed at immediate popularity, but his success was a kind of magic and was in any case largely ill-deserved. "The arts by which Pope . . . . contrived to procure to himself a more general and higher reputation than perhaps any English Poet ever attained during his life-time, are known to the judicious." His achievement was factitious: "he bewitched the nation by his melody, and dazzled it by his polished style". The success of Thomson's *Seasons* was even more complete and Wordsworth is happy to agree with a contemporary biographer that the work was "no sooner read than universally admired". Wordsworth admits that this case "appears to bear strongly against us"; but he is not without resource: "We must distinguish between wonder and legitimate admiration." Thomson's biographer was wrong; what he considered "genuine admiration must in fact have been blind wonderment". Between the publication of *Paradise Lost* (1667) and Thomson's *Seasons* (1726–30) scarcely a poem appeared which contained "a single new image of external nature". Thomson's accurate, fresh imagery came as an excellent novelty; but it was more the novelty than the excellence which appealed to men and caused them to wonder: "Wonder is the natural product of Ignorance; and as the soil was *in such good condition* at the time of the publication of the Seasons, the crop was doubtless abundant." The argument here is as confused as the imagery; the soil into which *The Seasons* dropped might have been more accurately described as a bad soil unlikely to foster the growth of Thomson's individual talent or secure for it a reading public. But, in any case, Wordsworth finds other reasons to explain his success: "Thomson was fortunate in the very title of his poem;" and then, of course, Thomson writes very badly and so was bound to have a wide appeal: "notwithstanding his high powers, he writes a vicious style; and his false ornaments are exactly of that kind which would be most likely to strike the undiscerning." His poems abound with "sentimental commonplaces" that have "an imposing air of novelty". You can tell that Thomson wasn't appreciated for the right reasons because "in any well-used copy of the Seasons the book generally opens of itself with the rhapsody on love, or with one of the stories". In fact there is no proof that "the true characteristics of Thomson's genius as an imaginative poet were perceived". After this hotchpotch of contradictory argument and special pleading Wordsworth claims that, in any case, Thomson *wasn't* appreciated in his own time, since possibly his best poem, *The Castle of Indolence*, "was neglected on its appearance, and is at this day the delight only of a few"! Not even posterity, it seems, is always to be trusted. Indeed the sins of omission in Johnson's *The Lives of the Poets* (no Spenser, no Sidney) prove the fickleness of posterity, and the sins of commission ("various metrical writers utterly worthless and useless") are "evidence what a small quantity of brain is necessary to procure a considerable stock of admiration, provided the aspirant will accommodate himself to the likings and fashions of his day". The object of Wordsworth's "hasty retrospect" has been to explain why he is not yet popular. To be rejected by the public of the day has been the fate of every great English poet since the Renaissance and "from the literature of other ages and other countries, proofs equally cogent might have been adduced". Wordsworth's rejection is not a sign of his singularity but a proof of his genius.

Coming more closely to the reception of his own poems since 1798 Wordsworth declares that he has cause to be satisfied: "The love, the admiration, the indifference, the slight, the aversion, and even the contempt, with which these Poems have been received" must all be taken as "pledges and tokens" and as "proofs that for the present time I have not laboured in vain". As we saw earlier, indifference, aversion and contempt are automatic proof that he has written well; love and admiration are the just reward and consolation from that tiny moral élite who alone throughout the ages have given recognition to the new prophet. Wordsworth's survey of literary history and the great poet's reception leads him to a further statement of that important principle which he had suggested in a letter some years earlier, "that every great author, as far as he is great and at the same time original, has had the task of *creating* the taste by which he is to be enjoyed: so has it been, so will it continue to be".[32]

Wordsworth's connection with earlier writers is not simply that he has shared their fate. He has a firm neo-classic sense of the great writer's indebtedness to the past, and he expresses it in terms close to those which T. S. Eliot uses in "Tradition and the Individual Talent" but which also indicate the tension in Wordsworth's position at the point where Renaissance and Romantic theory meet:

> The predecessors of an original Genius of high order will have smoothed the way for all that he has in common with them; – and much he will have in common; but, for what is peculiarly his own, he will be called upon to clear and often to shape his own road; – he will be in the condition of Hannibal among the Alps. (*Prose Works*, iii, p. 80)

The critical position is neo-classic, but the final image reveals the lonely originality of the Romantic poet. Posterity will be more likely to appreciate the "truly original poet" since he will have broken "the bonds of custom" which made earlier understanding difficult; he will have overcome previous "prejudices of false refinement" and will have made the Alps familiar to those who follow after. The great poet will widen "the sphere of human sensibility for the benefit of posterity", and in characteristically religious terms Wordsworth explains that the poet will establish "that dominion over the spirits of readers by which they are to be humbled and humanised, in order that they may be purified and exalted". Wordsworth quarrels with his own use of the word "taste"; it is unsatisfactory because it comes from "a *passive* sense of the human body" and is therefore inappropriate to poetry. For the reader of poetry must work with the poet; there must be "the exertion of a co-operating *power* in the mind of the Reader" if he is to be able to enter into "the pathetic and sublime" of poetry:

> Away, then, with the senseless iteration of the word, *popular*, applied to new works in poetry, as if there were no test of excellence in this first of the fine arts but that all men should run after its productions . . . (*Prose Works*, iii, p. 83)

Popular poetry will always be trivial and superficial and will appeal only to the curiosity or fancy of readers; but where poetry is acted upon by "the creative or abstracting virtue of the imagination" it will surely happen that "there, the poet must reconcile himself for a season to few and scattered hearers".

Yet even while Wordsworth states clearly the poet's inevitable isolation and prophetic role, he reaffirms that the poet is to keep alive the past for the future and so provide a continuity which, however taste may be modified, will gain for him an eventual great host of readers. The poet will show how

> the instinctive wisdom of antiquity and her heroic passions uniting, in the heart of the poet, with the meditative wisdom of later ages, have produced that accord of sublimated humanity, which is at once a history of the remote past and a prophetic enunciation of the remotest future. (Ibid.)

Once again Wordsworth projects on all great poets his own

Janus-like position at a meeting-point of two views of poetry, the
poet and his public. The reader of the *Essay* who has by now been
adequately assured that the fit audience of a great poet will be
very few and also that "there never has been a period, and
perhaps never will be, in which vicious poetry, of some kind or
other, has not excited more zealous admiration, and been far
more generally read, than good", might suppose that
Wordsworth had settled for an audience of a few today and for
posterity tomorrow, and might be inclined to answer "Yes" to
the rhetorical question with which Wordsworth begins his final
paragraph: "Is it the result of the whole, that, in the opinion of
the Writer, the judgement of the People is not to be respected?"
But, in fact, the answer is an emphatic "No" as Wordsworth
draws again his distinction between the Public and the People.
The People is not now simply a warmer word for Posterity but
hints consolingly at an acceptance of the poet in the less remote
future and helps the poet to evade the possible accusation of
contempt for his fellow-men. Good poetry, after all, survives:

> And how does it survive but through the People? What
> preserves it but their intellect and their wisdom?
>
> > '– Past and future, are the wings
> > On whose support, harmoniously conjoined,
> > Moves the great Spirit of human knowledge – '
>
> The voice that issues from this Spirit, is that Vox Populi which
> the Deity inspires. (*Prose Works*, iii, p. 84)

The voice that issues from the Public is quite a different thing;
there is no "divine infallibility in the clamour of that small
though loud portion of the community". The poet feels no
deference to this Public, but his "devout respect" and "reverence" are due to the People. It begins to look, however, as if
the People were a mysterious, possibly mystical and certainly
tenuous abstraction which does not actually consist of people.
The poet's respect and reverence are due to the People; that is,
"to the People, philosophically characterised, and to the em-

bodied spirit of their knowledge, so far as it exists and moves, at the present, faithfully supported by its two wings, the past and the future". Either this means nothing, or it is an appeal in different words to Johnson's common reader; "for by the common sense of readers uncorrupted with literary prejudices, after all the refinements of subtilty and the dogmatism of learning, must be finally decided all claim to practical honours".[33]

The tone of the *Essay, Supplementary to the Preface* reappears in letters of the same period. The many must remain for ever deaf to a great poet; for "a Soul that has been dwarfed by a course of bad culture cannot, after a certain age, be expanded into one of even ordinary proportion". The humble-minded alone can hope to understand Wordsworth's poetry although, as we saw, *The White Doe of Rylstone* in the same year was designed to be acceptable only to "the intelligent". Moral and poetic sensibility are inseparable. (Crabb Robinson suggested in 1812 that "Wordsworth is convinced that if men are to become better and wiser, the poems will sooner or later find their admirers".[34] At another time Wordsworth is caught in the circular argument that it is precisely the poems which will make men better and wiser.) In fact, if Miss Patty Smith can "read the description of Robert, and the fluctuations of hope and fear in Margaret's mind, and the gradual decay of herself and her dwelling without a bedimmed eye then I pity her"; and if she says that *The Excursion* is without passion, "then, thank Heaven! that the person so speaking is neither my wife nor my Sister, nor one whom (unless I could work in her a great alteration) I am forced to daily converse with".[35] Patty Smith on this showing would be incapable of reading the simplest epitaph since her "primary sensations" are "stifled" and her habits of reflection undeveloped. The good reader is also the good person. The poet will be able "to extend the domain of sensibility" of only those few readers "whose sensibility is already extended". Unto him that hath shall be given; for the have-nots Wordsworth despairs.

By 1815 Wordsworth has renounced the search for a public and has withdrawn into uncompromising aloofness; but by a strange irony his gradual withdrawal is accompanied and followed by a poetry more public in character and more popular, such as the "River Duddon" sonnets, most of *The Excursion* and the "Ecclesiastical Sonnets". If he gave up the public, the public did not, in the end, give up him. After 1815 Wordsworth said little more about the poet and his audience; the poet might continue to despair but the man worried shrewdly about his circulation and sales. In 1830 his publishers tell him that his buyers "are of that class who do not regard prices", but Wordsworth is not anxious for such buyers since his poetry "less than any other of the day is adapted to the taste of the luxurious". He worries that prices may reduce his sales and thinks that there might be an audience waiting to buy his works at a cheaper rate since the main body of his work "is as well fitted . . . to the bulk of the people both in sentiment and language, as that of any of my contemporaries". This astonishing remark is followed by the prophetic fear that "the perpetually supplied stimulus of Novels" will divert the interest of people from poetry. By 1833 he calmly accepts that there is not much "genuine relish" for poetry in Cumberland and that his own poems do not sell there; but he is still confident in 1835 that "Posterity will settle all accounts justly, and that works which deserve to last will last". The following year, 1836, he is "quite at ease" about the reception which his poems will have in the end. He had some reason for this relaxed confidence, for in 1838 he could tell Sir Robert Peel that he had "gained much more from my long-published writings within the last five or six years than in the thirty preceding". Financially this is good news, but he is still not sure if the right people are reading him for the right reasons. Miss Martineau assures him that his poems are in "the hearts of the American people. That is the place I would fain occupy among the People of these Islands". The place will not be easy to attain since the "abstract quality" of many of his poems will "not in *itself* recommend them to the mass of the people", although he is "not at all sure" that it will stand in the way of all the people. It didn't stand in the way of all the people. It is possibly to regret that the happy reconcilement of the poet and his public achieved in the *Essays upon Epitaphs* did not last, and at the same time to share the pleasure of the elderly Wordsworth's simple gratitude when he writes in 1840: "You will be pleased to learn that I frequently receive testimonies from Individuals who live by the labour of their hands, that what I have written has not been a dead letter to them."[36]

2 The Poet in Search of a Poem

> . . . even so didst thou become
> A *silent Poet* . . .
>
> . . . the habit of looking at things
> through the steady light of words.
>
> Wordsworth

I

Wordsworth was not only in search of a public; he was also in search of a poem. He believed that poetry must be artless, that the impressiveness of the subject as it is in Nature and in fact would be enough to make a poem, and that the poet "will feel that there is no necessity to trick out or elevate nature"; and at the same time he steadily saw the poet as artist and his poems as made things, the result of craft, workmanship and "long and deep thinking". He saw little in recent literature to persuade him that the task of resolving such opposite views of poetry would be an easy one. "In historical terms," say Professor Lindenberger,

> we might think of Wordsworth as veering between two irreconcilable literary systems: between the demands of decorum and the demands of sincerity, or . . . between the responsibilities imposed by the recognition of a hierarchy of styles and the responsibilities he felt to the truth of his personal experience.[1]

It is Wordsworth's achievement to have reconciled these irreconcilables, to have satisfied the opposing demands of Art or

47

Decorum and Sincerity and the rival notions of the poet as artist
and skylark. It has naturally been more usual to consider
Wordsworth's poetry and critical writings as a search for
sincerity; he is, after all, a great Romantic poet, and for many
readers his triumph is that, because he was a Romantic poet, he
ignored decorum and triumphed over art. This was how readers
wanted to see him, and they accepted his poems as (the phrase is
Wordsworth's) "breathings of simple nature". This partial view
was, and is, encouraged by Wordsworth's comments on spontaneity and by what is sometimes called his revolt against art,
against literature, against language itself.

If Wordsworth's intention and achievement are misinterpreted, the fault is partly his. The (repeated) remark that "poetry
is the spontaneous overflow of powerful feelings" is not the most
memorable statement in the Preface to *Lyrical Ballads* but it is the
most easily remembered. At the time it gave emphatic expression
to that growing prestige of the spontaneous which was one
characteristic of the Age of Sensibility. Spontaneity became a
guarantee of sincerity and encouraged a view of the poet and his
poems which is still current. Wordsworth's phrase, confirmed by
Shelley's image of the poet as skylark pouring forth his full heart
"In profuse strains of unpremeditated art", became a definition
of poetry and a description of what the poet did, or passively
allowed to happen. Literary history has been used to explain and
endorse Wordsworth's apparent emphasis on spontaneity and
what is thought to be his anti-literary stance. We know, for
example, that he had read Hugh Blair's *Lectures on Rhetoric* (1783)
and it is certainly possible to make out a case for Wordsworth's
indebtedness to these lectures. Blair says interesting, apposite
things:

> If we attend to the language that is spoken by persons under
> the influence of real passion, we shall find it always plain and
> simple; abounding indeed with those figures which express a
> disturbed and impetuous state of mind, such as interrogations,
> exclamations, and apostrophes; but never employing those
> which belong to the mere embellishment and parade of speech.

We never meet with any subtilty or refinement, in the sentiments of real passion. The thoughts which passion suggests, are always plain and obvious ones, arising directly from its object. Passion . . . expresses itself most commonly in short, broken, and interrupted speeches; corresponding to the violent and desultory emotions of the mind.[2]

Blair is here talking about the language appropriate to verse drama; closer to Wordsworth are some comments which express a primitivist view of poetry:

Poetry, however, in its ancient original condition, was perhaps more vigorous than it is in its modern state. It included then, the whole burst of the human mind; the whole exertion of its imaginative faculties. It spoke then the language of passion, and no other; for to passion it owed its birth. Prompted and inspired by objects which to him seemed great, by events which interested his country or his friends, the early bard arose and sung. He sung indeed in wild and disorderly strains; but they were the native effusions of his heart; they were the ardent conceptions of admiration or resentment, of sorrow or friendship, which he poured forth. It is no wonder, therefore, that in the rude and artless strain of the first poetry of all nations, we should often find somewhat that captivates and transports the mind. In after-ages, when poetry became a regular art, studied for reputation and for gain, authors began to affect what they did not feel. Composing coolly in their closets, they endeavoured to imitate passion, rather than to express it; they tried to force their imagination into raptures, or to supply the defect of native warmth, by those artificial ornaments which might give composition a splendid appearance.[3]

In the Golden Age there was no distinction between spontaneity and art. Poetry then was "artless" and for that reason still "captivates and transports" our minds. Poetry as "a regular art" brought down the curse of insincerity on its head ("authors began to affect what they did not feel") and instead of "effusions of the

heart" gave us poetic diction, "artificial ornaments" (the phrase
recalls Wordsworth's "gaudy and inane phraseology") which
"might give composition a splendid appearance". Elsewhere
Blair comes closer still to Wordsworth and insists that

> Almost every man, in passion, is eloquent. Then, he is at no loss
> for words and arguments. He transmits to others, by a sort of
> contagious sympathy, the warm sentiments which he feels: his
> looks and gestures are all persuasive; and nature shows herself
> infinitely more powerful than art.[4]

Here is the familiar stress on spontaneity, the belief that the
writer need not rely on language, but can communicate directly
by "contagious sympathy". Here is the denigration of art, and a
hint ("looks and gestures are all persuasive") that every man
(since all men will be sometimes in passion) is potentially a poet.

These things are close to Wordsworth, but they are not close
enough; Wordsworth's critical opinions are more intelligent,
subtle and shifting than anything in Blair. (Wordsworth's talk of
spontaneity is in part a rhetorical, even political, device.)
Random quotation from Wordsworth's critical writings can
shatter the balancing of opposing views he puts forward and the
synthesis he wins. Talk of poetry as "the spontaneous overflow
of powerful feelings" describes neither his own critical position
nor his poetic practice. The letters contain many references to
Wordsworth's revisions of his own work; Mary Wordsworth
complains that William had exhausted himself "by attempting
needless corrections". Dorothy Wordsworth's *Journals* make clear
the agony that attended the birth of many poems: "William all
the morning engaged in wearisome compositions"; "William
worked hard at *The Pedlar* and tired himself"; "Still at work at
The Pedlar, altering and refitting"; "William worked at *The
Ruined Cottage* and made himself very ill"; "William went to bed
tired with thinking about a poem"; "William very nervous. After
he was in bed, haunted with altering *The Rainbow*"; "William
tired himself with hammering at a passage". Wordsworth is
impatient when other poets claim spontaneity:

Milton talks of 'pouring easy his unpremeditated verse'. It would be harsh, untrue, and odious, to say there is anything like cant in this; but it is not true to the letter, and tends to mislead. (*LY*, ii, p. 586)

More interesting still is an oblique comment on the notion of unpremeditated or spontaneous verse in a letter written shortly after the death of his brother John:

> At first I had a strong impulse to write a poem that should record my Brother's virtues and be worthy of his memory. I began to give vent to my feelings, with this view, but I was over-powered by my subject and could not proceed: I composed much, but it is all lost except a few lines, as it came from me in such a torrent that I was unable to remember it. . . . This work must therefore rest awhile till I am something calmer . . . (*EY*, p. 586)

The final phrase, "till I am something calmer" takes us back to the Preface, and we find that when Wordsworth repeats that poetry is "the spontaneous overflow of powerful feelings" he adds that "it takes its origin from emotion recollected in tranquillity". The fame of this phrase almost conceals the paradox established by such a radical qualification of "spontaneous overflow".

The notion of "spontaneous overflow", then, is of little importance in the argument of the Preface and of no importance anywhere else; it is mentioned in the Preface merely to be modified and is afterwards abandoned. For Wordsworth the problem of sincerity is not to be solved by such a naive notion, and thereafter in the Preface and in all later comments the emphasis falls increasingly on the poet as "maker" and on the poem as a thing made. In a note to "The Thorn" (added, it is true, in 1843), he writes:

> Arose out of my observing, on the ridge of Quantock Hill, on a stormy day, a thorn which I had often passed in calm and bright weather without noticing it. I said to myself, 'Cannot I

by some invention do as much to make this Thorn permanently an impressive object as the storm has made it to my
eyes at this moment?' (*PW*, ii, p. 511)

Even for so notorious a poem Wordsworth is invoking the neo-
classic concept of Invention. All that remained after the Preface
was an occasional casual attempt (always in words marked by
neither spontaneity nor powerful feelings) to persuade the reader
that Wordsworth was composing spontaneously:

> . . . thus flowed my thoughts
> In a pure stream of words fresh from the heart.[5]

Spontaneity is clearly a convention. After the first reference to it
in the Preface Wordsworth adds that "Poems to which any value
can be attached were never produced on any variety of subjects
but by a man who, being possessed of more than usual organic
sensibility, had also thought long and deeply."

Wordsworth does not claim in the Preface that spontaneity
will be achieved by the poet's using "the real language of men",
even when men are in a state of "vivid sensation". He insists on
"a selection of the real language of men". This selection will be
made "with true taste" and "will entirely separate the composition from the vulgarity and meanness of ordinary life"; it will
remove "what would otherwise be painful or disgusting in the
passion". But selection, it seems, can also include additions.
Wordsworth's principle

> had been to give the oral part as nearly as he could in the very
> words of the speakers, where he narrated a real story,
> dropping, of course, all vulgarisms or provincialisms, and
> borrowing sometimes a Bible turn of expression: these former
> were mere accidents, not essential to the truth in representing
> how the human heart and passions worked; and to give these
> last faithfully was his object.[6]

(Scott believed that ordinary men and women "under the

influence of passion" would themselves use "Bible turns of expression", and he illustrated this in Jeanie Deans's appeal to the queen.) Wordsworth seldom uses the unselected language of men, but one such use occurs in "Simon Lee". In a note to the poem Wordsworth claims that "The expression when the hounds were out, 'I dearly love their voices' was word for word from his own lips".[7] Another is the opening line of the poem "Stepping Westward". Wordsworth tells that while he and Dorothy were walking by the side of Loch Katrine "we met, in one of the loneliest parts of that solitary region, two well-dressed Women, one of whom said to us, by way of greeting, 'What, you are stepping westward?' "[8] The real undiluted, unselected language of men could not usually, it seems, serve a rhetorical purpose; through it Wordsworth was not able to control the reader's response.

In a letter of 1808 Wordsworth scorns the idea of spontaneity. He refers to the death of two neighbours, George and Sarah Green, who had fallen over a precipice in Langdale:

> Within a day or two after my return home, when my mind was easier than it has been since, in passing through the church-yard I stopped at the grave of the poor Sufferers and immediately afterwards composed the following stanzas; *composed* I have said. I ought rather to have said effused, for it is the mere pouring out of my own feeling . . . (*MY*, i, p. 219)

Poetry is composition, not effusion; the word "mere" supports what he says in the Preface, but confounds his flirtation with the notion of spontaneity and popular interpretations of what he said. Wordsworth's dilemma is there again and again in the Preface. It would, he says, be easy to prove to the reader

> that not only the language of a large portion of every good poem even of the most elevated character, must necessarily, except with reference to the metre, in no respect differ from that of good prose, but likewise that some of the most

> interesting parts of the best poems will be found to be strictly
> the language of prose when prose is well written. (*Prose Works*,
> i, p. 133)

Wordsworth's discussion of metre is notorious. Poetry is the same
as prose, but *not* the same as prose; words like "large portion" and
"some" leave escape routes open. Prose which is "well written"
would seem to be a selection of the language really used by men.
Poetry is spontaneous, and yet, because of metre, at two removes
from this real language of men. A few lines earlier Wordsworth
writes: "I have at all times endeavoured to look steadily at my
subject; consequently, there is I hope in these Poems little
falsehood of description . . ." The literal-minded Wordsworth
will, it seems, fit word to thing without the intervention of art; but
after a comma art reappears in the form of Decorum, with the
words "and my ideas are expressed in language fitted to their
respective importance". The fact that metrical language is better
fitted than prose to express the truth makes plain the ambiguity
in the meaning of "language" as Wordsworth uses it; sometimes he
means merely vocabulary, but at other times he seems to mean
speech-patterns and rhythm. Wordsworth may often use the
language really used by men, but not in the way men use it.
Certainly, his discussion of metre makes impossible any ordinary
interpretation of spontaneity. Metre offers the delight of likeness
in difference; it offers "an indistinct perception perpetually
renewed of language closely resembling that of real life and yet,
in the circumstance of metre, differing from it so widely".

The dilemma of language and metre extends to form as well (a
more familiar dilemma to Romantic and post-Romantic poets).
In the sestet of a sonnet Wordsworth asks and (almost angrily)
answers the question

> How does the Meadow-flower its bloom unfold?
> Because the lovely little flower is free
> Down to its root, and, in that freedom, bold;
> And so the grandeur of the Forest-tree
> Comes not by casting in a formal mould,
> But from its *own* divine vitality.

The writer who rejects organic form ("its *own* divine vitality") for traditional verse forms is no poet but a "groveller":

A POET! – He hath put his heart to school,
Nor dares to move unpropped upon the staff
Which Art hath lodged within his hand – must laugh
By precept only, and shed tears by rule.
Thy Art be Nature; the live current quaff,
And let the groveller sip his stagnant pool . . . (*PW*, iii, p. 52)

Art is the opposite of Nature, and a failure in spontaneity is a failure in sincerity ("shed tears by rule"); but all this is being expressed in a sonnet, that most formal of moulds which found in Wordsworth (and not only the later Wordsworth) one of its greatest practitioners. The sonnet is undated. In another sonnet (also undated) Wordsworth comes to the defence of Form:

Scorn not the Sonnet; Critic, you have frowned,
Mindless of its just honours; with this key
Shakespeare unlocked his heart; the melody
Of this small lute gave ease to Petrarch's wound . . . (*PW*, iii,
    p. 20)

Art is no longer opposed to Nature. In a rigid verse-form the heart can be unlocked; the demands of art and sincerity can be met, although this will not be Wordsworth's usual way of meeting them.

In a letter of 1816 Wordsworth finds a semantic solution to the rigid opposition of spontaneity or Nature and Art, and a way to reconcile them:

Sir E. is quite correct in stating that no Poetry can be good without animation. But when he adds, 'that the position will almost exclude whatever is very highly and artificially laboured, for great sacrifice must destroy animation', he thinks laxly and uses words inconsiderately. – Substitute for the word 'artificially' the word, 'artfully', and you will at once see that nothing can be more erroneous than the assertion. The word, 'artificially' begs the question, because that word is always employed in an unfavourable sense. Gray failed as a Poet, not because he took too much pains, and so extinguished his animation; but because he had little of that fiery quality to begin with; and his pains were of the wrong sort. (*MY*, ii, p. 301)

It is true that as Wordsworth grew older the manner of his poems changed, and it is true that in his comments on poetry he came to lay more stress on poetry as an art, as craft and (a later favourite word) workmanship; but this change is not a simple movement from Nature towards Art, since he had never fully accepted so firm a distinction. In the *Essays upon Epitaphs* (to which I shall return) Art is still the "adversary" of Nature, and yet Wordsworth sees no reason why an epitaph should not have "beauty of language" and "sweetness of versification". Spontaneity has no place in an epitaph. The epitaph is very much an example of "emotion recollected in tranquillity", for "an Epitaph presupposes a Monument upon which it is to be engraven", and "to raise a monument is a sober and reflective act". The writer of an epitaph "is bound in this case, more than in any other, to give proof that he himself has been moved"; but proof of his sincerity will be achieved not by spontaneity, but by a control at once moral and aesthetic: "The passions should be subdued, the emotions controlled; strong, indeed, but nothing ungovernable or wholly involuntary. Seemliness requires this, and truth requires it also . . ." "Errors in taste and judgement" make a bad epitaph; a good epitaph, because it is art, is seemly and passionate; its "composition is a perfect whole; there is nothing arbitrary or mechanical, but it is an organised body of which the members are bound together by a common life and are all justly proportioned."[9]

In the Preface of 1815 Wordsworth lists a number of "powers requisite for the production of poetry", the last of which,

Judgement, will decide "how and where, and in what degree, each of these faculties ought to be exerted". But Judgement turns out to be Decorum, for it must determine "what are the laws and appropriate graces of every species' of composition". In 1814 Wordsworth writes that "My first expressions I often find detestable". In 1815 he much prefers the "*Classical* mode of Dr Beattie to the insupportable slovenliness" of Hogg and Scott, and by the following year "Multa *tulit* fecitque, must be the motto of all those who are to last". In 1821 he compliments W. S. Landor on having written "verses of which I would rather have been the Author than of any produced in our time", and he uses with approval the eighteenth-century critical term "strength" (defined by Johnson as "much meaning in few words").[10] In 1827 he writes to William Rowan Hamilton:

> you will be brought to acknowledge that the logical faculty has infinitely more to do with poetry than the young and inexperienced, whether writer or critic, ever dreams of. Indeed, as the materials upon which that faculty is exercised in poetry are so subtle, so plastic, so complex, the application of it requires an adroitness which can proceed from nothing but practice; a discernment, which emotion is so far from bestowing that at first it is ever in the way of it. (*LY*, i, p. 275)

He exhorts Hamilton and his sister to fix their attention on "those writers who have stood the test of time". In 1828 he talks of the "rules of art and workmanship which must be applied to imaginative literature, however high the subject, if it is to be permanently efficient". Miss Rowan Hamilton's verses have "spirit and feeling", but they lack workmanship, which is something "incalculably great". Poetry is "infinitely more of an art than the world is disposed to believe". This increasing emphasis on rules and craft may seem a sad falling away from that reconciliation of sincerity and art which he achieved in the *Essays upon Epitaphs*, but it cannot be dismissed as a hardening of Wordsworth's poetic arteries. Nearly all the later comments come from his letters, and their emphasis depends on his correspondents, many of whom had submitted their poems to him for criticism. Nevertheless Wordsworth can constantly surprise by the vigorous contradictions which show that the dilemma of sincerity and art, and the difficulty of their reconcilement, engaged him to the end. In 1830, for example, he writes in a letter:

> Your Poem is vigorous, and that is enough for me – I think it in some places diffuse, in others somewhat rugged, from the originality of your mind. You feel strongly; trust to those feelings, and your poem will take its shape and proportions as a tree does from the vital principle that actuates it. I do not think that great poems can be cast in a mould. – Homer's, the greatest of all, certainly was not. Trust, again I say, to yourself. (*LY*, i, p. 537)

It is worth noting that the word "mould" can mean two different things for Wordsworth. In the sonnet I quoted earlier it seemed to mean simply "form", in that case a sonnet; and since the same phrase is used again in this letter (the same image, too: perhaps the sonnet was written at the same time) it might be assumed to mean, again, "form". But in the Preface of 1815 Wordsworth tries to distinguish between "form" and "mould". "The materials of Poetry . . . are cast, by means of various moulds, into divers forms." The various moulds are "the Narrative", "the Dramatic", "the Lyrical", "the Idyllium", "Didactic" and "philosophical Satire". Each mould includes several forms; the Idyllium, for example, includes (among others) the Epitaph, the Inscription and the Sonnet. It is not in a letter but in a considered note on one of his poems that Wordsworth in 1843 comments for the last time on the question of sincerity. He asks with reference to Petrarch:

> Is it not in fact obvious that many of his love verses must have flowed, I do not say from a wish to display his own talent, but from a habit of exercising his intellect in that way rather than from an impulse of his heart?[11]

2

If Wordsworth's talk of spontaneity is sometimes seen as an attack on literature, his concern with the larger question of sincerity has in recent years been called an attack on language itself. Helen Darbishire writes:

> Wordsworth's was a revolt of a nature and importance which perhaps no literary revolt had before. It was a revolt against literature, and assertion of the supreme value of life at all cost in poetry.[12]

Another critic finds proof of this opposition of literature and life, words and truth, in Wordsworth's remark in the Preface to *Lyrical Ballads* that no words which the poet's "fancy or imagination can suggest, will be to be compared with those which are the emanations of reality and truth". Such emanations are, of course, also words, but words uttered (not written) "by men in real life under the actual pressure of . . . passions". Wordsworth does not suggest that reality and truth can be revealed by inarticulateness, by grunts and groans; even here the apparent rejection of words is not absolute. This distrust of language (especially written language) and the belief that words are not simply feeble vehicles for truth but may not be able to carry truth at all, is very old and very modern. In the *Phaedrus* Socrates by a myth condemns the invention of writing. The written word provides a show of wisdom without the reality; through writing, people will seem to possess much knowledge, but for the most part they know nothing at all (275). Socrates opposes to this the superiority of the spoken word, dialectic, "the wise man's discourse, which is possessed both of life and soul, and of which the written one may fairly be called the shadow" (276). The written word cannot teach the truth; only through the spoken word can we reach what is really worthy of attention and write it in "the soul of the hearer" (278). In the *Seventh Letter* Plato is even more emphatic, and his pessimism about the written word now extends to all language: "No man of intelligence will venture to express his philosophical

views in language, especially not in language that is unchange-
able, which is true of that which is set down in written
characters" (343a). Words can even come between a man and
the truth, and when the soul is seeking to know the very essence of
a thing words can fill the soul with "puzzlement and perplexity"
(343c). A man's audience may sometimes feel that he knows
nothing of the things on which he is trying to write or speak, for
they are not aware that it is not the mind of the writer or speaker
which is at fault but "the defective nature" of language (343d).
Through dialectic, "the scrutiny and kindly testing by men who
proceed by question and answer without ill will" (344b), there
may sometimes come, with a sudden flash, understanding about
every problem; but a wise man, when he deals with important
things, "will be far from exposing them to ill feeling and
misunderstanding among men by committing them to writing"
(344c). What a man values, the things of greatest worth, are laid
up silently in his heart (344d). In the *Phaedrus* Socrates tells his
audience ironically that in ancient days men "not being clever
like you moderns, were content, in their simplicity, to listen to an
oak or a stone, if only it spoke the truth" (275).

This unease with language has often appeared in great
literature; Cordelia knows that her love is "more ponderous"
than her tongue and she must therefore "love and be silent". But
neither Plato nor Shakespeare considers words as an enemy of
sincerity. "Sincere" and "sincerity" are words which Shakespeare scarcely ever uses, and only once in *King Lear*. The
word "sincerity" had not yet come to mean a special form of
truth, something more private, more subjective, more linked to
personality. In *Mansfield Park* the change is beginning. Fanny
Price is (notoriously) a poor talker. She is usually silent in
company and she frequently retires to her little room to be more
silent still. Her longest speech comes when she speaks "her
feelings" and tells us that if the natural world were attended to,
people would be "carried more out of themselves"; and at the
end of the scene we read that "Fanny sighed alone at the
window" (Chapter 11). When we come to Fanny's "real and
substantial action and suffering" (the phrase is Wordsworth's) in

the scene where Sir Thomas Bertram tries to bully her into marrying Henry Crawford, Fanny cannot find more than the few, bare, necessary words to explain her refusal: "I – I cannot like him, Sir, well enough to marry him" (Chapter 32). Her stammer and her many silences authenticate her truth-seeing: "I was quiet, but I was not blind." All this, of course, is to contrast with Mary Crawford, who uses language to conceal the truth about herself by creating a false image of herself (insincerity); her words are not inadequate but are adequate only for falsehood. In short, she uses words as art and not as "the emanations of truth and nature". More recent assaults on language have emphasised this connection between language and insincerity. For Sartre words not only obscure the truth of things but lead to *mauvaise foi*; the final sincerity is silence.

But in Wordsworth there is no revolt against language; there is no assault on the word. A successful revolt against language ends in silence, and Wordsworth was never silent unless we except, perhaps, the years 1793–6, his dark years. In this period he may, indeed, have undergone a revolt against language; but since he did not (and by the nature of things, could not) write about it, we can only guess at the reason for his silence. At this point the paradoxes threaten to flow thick and fast and unprofitably. It is enough to say that when he collaborated with Coleridge on *Lyrical Ballads* the revolt, if there was one, was over and that in the very different poems of the second (1800) edition all trace of it was gone. Wordsworth's famous rejection of "gaudy and inane phraseology" is not a rejection of language; and his statement in the Preface that humble and rustic life was generally chosen as the subject of his poems because for people in that condition "the essential passions of the heart find a better soil in which they can attain their maturity . . . and speak a plainer and more emphatic language", is not the only thing he said about language or the possibility of finding a language adequate to the burdens of truth and sincerity.

Wordsworth's discussion of the adequacy of language is found almost entirely in the Preface to *Lyrical Ballads* and in the *Essays upon Epitaphs*. These writings, particularly the *Essays*, are his "intolerable wrestle with words" and in them are his most extreme and pessimistic statements on the possibilities of language. But this does not mean that they can be plundered for quotations to prove an attack on literature and language; nor is it possible on the strength (or weakness) of such quotations to turn Wordsworth into a modern or find him the depressed prophet of all contemporary retreats from the word. Evidence for Wordsworth's defeatism is sought in his famous silent solitaries, in the Old Cumberland Beggar, the Old Man Travelling, the Discharged Soldier, the Leech-gatherer. But it is misleading to say that in them "even language has lost its power of life",[13] for (paradoxically) the poems in which they appear superbly articulate silence; if the language of these solitaries has lost its life, the language of the poems has life and has it more abundantly. Preface and *Essays* vigorously examine the possibility and impossibility of language, and Wordsworth reconciles these opposites to find that language, and not simply the language of passion supposedly spoken by men in humble and rustic life, but a written, literary language (language as art) need be no barrier to truth, but can become the very language of truth. "Language became his central weapon against literary convention";[14] art and sincerity could be reconciled.

The first radical disquiet with language comes in the Preface, and some sentences have been eagerly seized on by critics who are intrigued by the seeming paradox of a great articulator recommending silence, a mighty poet turning his back on words, and who have wondered at this dreadful *trahison des clercs*. (At least one critic has found this recommendation to silence infectious and (almost) compelling. In her Preface to her Clark Lectures for 1949 on *The Poet Wordsworth* Helen Darbishire writes: "I had thought that I should never again talk or write about Wordsworth (so thoroughly had I learnt among the hills his lesson of silence) – but . . ." but luckily she did go on to write about Wordsworth again in the lectures which followed.)

Wordsworth puts forward opposing views. The "What is a Poet?" passage, which was added to the Preface in 1802 and which redresses the greater gloom of the first edition, endows the poet with mighty qualities, though insisting that he is a man speaking to men. Among these qualities are

> a greater readiness and power in expressing what he thinks and feels, and especially those thoughts and feelings which, by his own choice, or from the structure of his own mind, arise in him without immediate external excitement. (*Prose Works*, i, p. 138)

And yet this Poet, this mighty mountain, is, it seems, to bring forth a mouse:

> But whatever portion of this faculty [that is, the poet's power already referred to] we may suppose even the greatest Poet to possess, there cannot be a doubt that the language which it will suggest to him, must often, in liveliness and truth, fall short of that which is uttered by men in real life, under the actual pressure of those passions, certain shadows of which the Poet thus produces, or feels to be produced in himself. (Ibid.)

The Platonic imagery and distrust are interesting; the words which men utter in real life when they are moved by passions are the ideal Forms, and the poet's words mere shadows of them. The poet sees through a glass darkly, and the glass is words; men stirred by passion enable us to see truth face-to-face. This truth, of course, is still mediated by words, but by words which are at once all-powerful, transparent and (Wordsworth seems to suggest) scarcely necessary. But for all the vivid phrases Wordsworth is more cautious than his critics. Helen Darbishire quotes the above passage and some lines which follow shortly after:

> However exalted a notion we would wish to cherish of the character of a Poet, it is obvious that while he describes and imitates passions, his employment is in some degree mechanical, compared with the freedom and power of real and substantial action and suffering. (Ibid.)

She then asks:

> Has any other poet at any time held this perverse belief that
> poetry has *less* freedom and power to express human feeling
> than the human actors and sufferers themselves whose ex-
> perience the poet tries to render?[15]

The answer to the question is "No; not even always
Wordsworth". When Roger Sharrock says of this same passage
that "A pessimism so bleak about the possibilities of poetic
language could not be sustained for long by any writer who was
to go on writing", he is right: the pessimism, as we shall see,
disappears in the next sentence.

Much depends on what version of the Preface is used. My
quotations come from *Poetical Works* (London, 1850). In the
second passage quoted the word "often" was first inserted in 1845
and thus largely contradicts the earlier version. In general the
various changes which Wordsworth in later editions made at this
point in the argument heavily qualify the earlier dogmatism and
bleakness. A sharp change has been made in the third extract
from the Preface. In 1845 Wordsworth substituted the words "in
some degree mechanical" for the earlier words "altogether
slavish and mechanical", and it was the emphasis of this phrase
which led to Helen Darbishire's question. It might, of course, be
argued that these later changes should be discounted as the
defensive caution of a much older man who had reached quiet
waters and was embarrassed by his earlier critical excesses. The
argument is, I believe, untenable but, luckily, need not be
pursued, since the qualification was already there in 1802 and
came in the next sentence. The poet who takes the language
"which is uttered by men in real life, under the actual pressure
of . . . passions", will have one task, that of

> modifying only the language which is thus suggested to him by
> a consideration that he describes for a particular purpose, that
> of giving pleasure. Here, then, he will apply the principle of
> selection which has already been insisted upon. He will depend

upon this for removing what would otherwise be painful or disgusting in the passion . . . (Ibid, pp. 138–9)

What is remarkable here in the Preface is not the pessimism but the careful, subtle balancing (it is not yet a reconcilement) of opposites. Wordsworth insists always on the high responsibilities of the poet towards the language he uses and on what he refers to as "the dignity of his art". The reader of the Preface is reminded – and the phrase is in every revision and edition – that "the powers of language are not so limited as he may suppose".

3

It is the *Essays upon Epitaphs* (especially the second and third) which might seem to contain Wordsworth's most extreme comments on the inadequacy of language and his most sombre thinking on words, sincerity and silence. It is not simply that in these essays he wonders how he may write "a poem which affects not to be poetry" (the phrase is Coleridge's), for in that case the poetry would be in the affecting. That was roughly his position in the Preface. Now he faces the dilemma that the poet is a truth-teller who uses words, and yet "Words are too awful an instrument for good and evil to be trifled with; they hold above all other external powers a dominion over thoughts". The biblical echoes in "powers" and "dominion" suggest the mighty authority and force of language. Words are "an incarnation of thought", and he continues:

> Language, if it do not uphold, and feed, and leave in quiet, like the power of gravitation or the air we breathe, is a counter-spirit, unremittingly and noiselessly at work to derange, to subvert, to lay waste, to vitiate, and to dissolve. (*Prose Works*, ii, p. 85)

No other romantic poet has such veneration for words. Byron found Wordsworth much too literary a poet, and in a way he was right; in its traditional emphasis on the power of the Word this

comment of Wordsworth's is an echo of *The Dunciad*, where Pope
shows in the scribblers how language can "derange", "subvert"
and "lay waste".

> Round him much Embryo, much Abortion lay,
> Much future Ode, and abdicated Play;
> Nonsense precipitate, like running Lead,
> That slip'd thro' Cracks and Zig-zags of the Head;
> All that on Folly Frenzy could beget,
> Fruits of dull Heat, and Sooterkins of Wit . . .
> Here lay poor Fletcher's half-eat scenes, and here
> The Frippery of crucify'd Moliere . . .

The goddess of Dulness dramatises language as counter-spirit in
the final allusion of the poem:

> Lo! thy dead Empire, CHAOS! is restor'd;
> Light dies before they uncreating word . . .[16]

And yet Wordsworth finds that the most impressive of all
epitaphs had almost dispensed with language; on "a very small
stone" was nothing but the name of an infant and the dates of his
birth and death which revealed that he had "been born one day
and died the following".

Much of the sharpness of Wordsworth's dilemma comes from
conflicting views of the relation between language and thought
or feeling. "An experienced and well-regulated mind" will not
object to the "monotonous language of sorrow and affectionate
admiration" which he finds on tombstones; such language is a
"veil" which covers "a substance of individual truth". "Upon all
men, and upon such a mind in particular, an Epitaph must strike
with a gleam of pleasure, when the expression is of that kind
which carries conviction t the heart at once that the Author was a
sincere mourner." Sincerity, then, can be achieved by monotonous (that is, unvariegated and frequently repeated) language.
It is not clear whether the "gleam of pleasure" (Wordsworth

always insisted that the poet's first task was to give pleasure) is the pleasure given by art, or the pleasure of meeting old familiar phrases yet again, or the moral pleasure which results from coming face-to-face with sincerity. This sincerity may be achieved "by a naked ejaculation", but the example which Wordsworth gives (a translation of a German epitaph) does not make the matter clear: "Ah! they have laid in the Grave a brave Man – he was to me more than many!"[17] This is scarcely a "naked ejaculation"; the two halves, the fact and the response to it, the public statement and the private reaction, are balanced, as they are in the final lines of "She dwelt among the untrodden ways":

> But she is in her grave, and, oh,
> The difference to me!

The language of the German epitaph and of Wordsworth's lines is not monotonous; the sincerity (the poetry) is not in the fact but in the art (the words). The poetry may be in the pity, but the pity is in the words. But by the term "ejaculation" Wordsworth may mean simply the opening "Ah" and the final exclamation mark. If he does, he is wrong, for the "gleam of pleasure" is not to be found in such minimal (wordless) communication. (Wordsworth is here at his furthest from Dr Johnson: "I think it may be observed that the particle O! used at the beginning of a sentence always offends".)[18] "An effect as pleasing", Wordsworth continues, "is often produced by the recital of an affliction endured with fortitude." If he means that the only words needed to move us are those which sparely record the facts, then we must recall that when he wrote such a tale ("The Ruined Cottage") he did more than recite the affliction of Margaret. (Her story is a matter of fact but it is not matter-of-fact.) If "the truth is weighty" in an epitaph, "the rudeness of expression" will not matter, although an epitaph may well contain a kind of bonus in "beauty of language" and "sweetness of versification". Unless we already share the beliefs on which an epitaph is built we shall never find it interesting; we shall never "arrive at that state or disposition of mind" necessary to make it thoroughly felt — (the good reader makes the good epitaph).

Wordsworth goes further; he finds that the anti-literary (or failed literary) qualities of some epitaphs, the "homeliness" of their language, the strangeness of their images, the "grotesque spelling" and "the quaint jingle of rhymes" are no bar to sincerity and truth, but "proof of how deeply the piety of the rude Forefathers of the hamlet is seated in their natures". Failure in an epitaph comes from the intrusion of language, when the writer fails to keep his eye steadily on his subject but prides himself on "what he might call a clever hit"[19] and is led astray by vanity; it comes, that is, from insincerity, and epitaphs raise the question of sincerity more urgently than any other "mode of composition":

> These suggestions may be further useful to establish a criterion of sincerity, by which a Writer may be judged; and this is of high import. For, when a Man is treating an interesting subject, or one which he ought not to treat at all unless he be interested, no faults have such a killing power as those which prove that he is not in earnest, that he is acting a part, has leisure for affectation, and feels that without it he could do nothing. This is one of the most odious of faults; because it shocks the moral sense: and is worse in a sepulchral inscription, precisely in the same degree as that mode of composition calls for sincerity more urgently than any other. And indeed, where the internal evidence proves that the Writer was moved, in other words where this charm of sincerity lurks in the language of a Tombstone and secretly pervades it, there are no errors in style or manner for which it will not be, in some degree, a recompence; but without habits of reflection a test of this inward simplicity cannot be come at: and, as I have said, I am now writing with a hope to assist the well-disposed to attain it. (*Prose Works*, ii, p. 70)

The echo of Dr Johnson's objection to "Lycidas" ("where there is leisure for fiction there is little grief") makes clear Wordsworth's very different bias. Language is now something separate from "style or manner"; the language of an epitaph can be without decorum, without art. And yet the qualification, "in some degree", opens the door again to let art in; there can be something better – and not less sincere – than the language really used by men. But literary art (the example Wordsworth gives is an instance of hyperbole in some funeral verses written by the Marquis of Montrose on the execution of Charles I) is sometimes "a mean instrument made mighty because wielded by an afflicted soul". If we ask how in this case we know that the poet is sincere, that he is an afflicted soul, the answer seems to be biographical and historical; we know that Montrose was a heroic soldier, that he was the sort of man who therefore *must* have been deeply moved. The hyperbolic language confirms the sincerity but does not create it, although Wordsworth, perpetually honest, admits that the epitaph is "instinct with spirit, and every word has its separate life".[20] But it is better to avoid "the more remote regions of illustrative imagery":

> For the occasion of writing an Epitaph is matter of fact in its intensity, and forbids more authoritatively than any other species of composition all modes of fiction, except those which the very strength of passion has created; which have been acknowledged by the human heart, and have become so familiar that they are converted into substantial realities. (*Prose Works*, ii, p. 76)

The paradoxical phrase "matter of fact in its intensity" marvellously describes the good epitaph and also many of Wordsworth's most characteristic poems. By "fiction" he means "illustrative imagery" (such imagery must always "elevate, deepen, or define the human passion"). What he recommends are phrases which have been so hallowed by tradition and time (many examples· can be found in the Bible and the *Book of Common Prayer*) that they cease to distract or obstruct the reader and become the very things which the words denote. This is not an attack on language but an assertion of its power, an assertion of language as incarnation.

The bare fact is important but it is not enough. Wordsworth disagrees with Dr Johnson over one of Pope's epitaphs, "On Mrs. Corbet, Who dyed of a Cancer in her Breast".[21] He lists the many faults of the epitaph but adds with his usual honest caution, "The Epitaph now before us owes what exemption it may have from these defects in its general plan to the excruciating disease of which the Lady died". The poetry of the epitaph comes (a little) from the situation as well as from the words, and epitaphs have the advantage of dealing with the most brutally matter-of-fact of all situations. But if Mrs Corbet had died, say, of pneumonia, Wordsworth feels that the total poem would have been even worse; because it was cancer the fact could a little redeem the fiction. In 1808 Wordsworth objected to Crabbe's *The Parish Register* (1807) because the poem seemed to rely too much on mere facts to achieve pathos. Telling the facts is not the same as telling the truth, and calling his picture true to nature is no defence:

> After all, if the Picture were true to nature, what claim would it have to be called Poetry? . . . The sum of all is, that nineteen out of 20 of Crabbe's Pictures are mere matters of fact; with which the Muses have just about as much to do as they have with a Collection of medical reports, or of Law cases. (*MY*, i, p. 268)

It is inevitable that an epitaph should contain thoughts and feelings which are "common-place, and even trite"; but the writer must present the common truths which are the staple of all epitaphs with "such accompaniment as shall imply that he has mounted to the source of things"; he must, that is, by throwing over things of every day a "colouring of imagination" teach us, in Shelley's phrase, "to imagine what we know". The most needful and difficult thing in an epitaph is "to give to universally received truths a pathos and a spirit which shall re-admit them into the soul like revelations of the moment."[22]

At other times Wordsworth keeps separate the language which expresses thoughts and the thoughts themselves; there is the implication that somehow there can be thinking without words. He complains that in one epitaph "the thoughts have their nature changed and moulded by the vicious expression in which they are entangled". In a cancelled passage in the second *Essay* Wordsworth finds that a writer's expression may be "thoroughly defiled and clogged" by contemporary poetic practice; "yet still through the force of circumstances that have roused him, his underfeeling may remain strong and pure. Yet this may be wholly concealed from common view".[23] (The repetition of "yet" catches Wordsworth's cautious handling of a difficult subject.) But if the "underfeeling" is concealed from common view, if it is not in the words, how do we know it is there, and where else could it possibly be? In the third *Essay* Wordsworth points out the two possible faults in the writing of an epitaph: there may be either no "current of just thought and feeling" at all, or a surface of "illustrative imagery" may either conceal or falsify such thought and feeling. But again, if it is concealed or falsified how can we know it is there or that it ever existed? If, in an epitaph, sincerity, "the unction of a devout heart, be wanting everything else is of no avail". But how shall we know if it is really wanting or only concealed? How can this 'unction' show itself except in words? Wordsworth's two answers to these questions may appear to contradict each other. One answer we have already seen: the bare facts of the case, a loved one dead and his loss lamented, and the bare situation, "the recital of an affliction endured with fortitude", are enough (when expressed in the most naked language possible) to transmit to the reader the pathos and the sincerity which must be there simply because the facts recited are the recurring tragedies of life and we, being men, must feel them. The other answer comes in a comment on an epitaph where the bare facts and the recital are more than usually moving; a father writes an epitaph on his own dead daughter:

Unquestionably, as the Father . . . speaks in his own Person, the situation is much more pathetic; but, making due allowance for this advantage, who does not here feel a superior truth and sanctity, which is not dependent upon this circumstance, but merely the result of the expression and the connection of the thoughts? (*Prose Works*, ii, p. 86)

It is language and art which (Wordsworth says) here reveal the truth and sincerity of the epitaph. Yet only a few pages later he can invite the reader to approve of the following epitaph from a country churchyard:

At the last day I'm sure I shall appear
To meet with Jesus Christ my Saviour dear,
Where I do hope to live with him in bliss;
Oh, what a joy in my last hour was this! (*Prose Works*, ii, p. 92)

It is pointless to protest that these four lines of jingle have no merit as poetry, that the naked ejaculation of the final line is not carried or earned by the earlier lines or that the bare facts are here not bare enough. Wordsworth's defence of the epitaph, like his defence of those poems in *Lyrical Ballads* which were mocked and and derided, is at the same time an attack on the reader. The spirit of the lines is not in the words; a reader's ability to discover and enter into the spirit "must depend upon his feeling, his imagination and his understanding". Such verses are saved from triviality by "the matter" (Wordsworth's phrase) and the matter of the verses (the facts) "can excite thought or feeling in the Reader". The most terrible poignancy of the infant's gravestone springs from nothing but name, date of birth and, one day later, date of death.

  J. W. Mackail, in his Introduction to *Select Epigrams from the Greek Anthology*[24] says helpful things about the necessary simplicity of the best Greek epitaphs and about the nature of that simplicity. The Greek epigram was "in its essence and origin" an inscriptional poem or epitaph. ("The Greek word 'epigram' in its original meaning is precisely equivalent to the Latin word 'inscription'.") These earlier inscriptions were nearly always epitaphs or dedications, and "if they went beyond a mere name or set of names, or perhaps the bare statement of a simple fact, were necessarily in verse"; "lapidary precision" or "imaginative tension" was needed to give the writing "directness and force". The epitaph, then, was a short poem; it was merely a convention to suppose that it must be actually inscribed or engraved on stone, but it "must have the compression and conciseness of a real inscription, and in proportion to the smallness of its bulk must be highly finished, even balanced, simple and lucid." Its simplicity goes with its art. Mackail finds the epitaphs of Simonides the finest of all. He quotes one on young Athenians who had died in battle, "Having died they are not dead", and on this and others he comments: "There are no superlatives. The emotion is kept strictly in the background, neither expressed nor denied."[25] Emotion "kept strictly" anywhere in a poem is kept there by art. As we saw earlier Wordsworth had declared that "The passions in an Epitaph should be subdued, the emotions controlled; strong indeed, but nothing ungovernable or wholly involuntary. Seemliness requires this, and truth requires it also: for how can the narrator otherwise be trusted". In the Simonides epitaph, "Having died they are not dead", the reader's pleasure comes from the art which offers him, in Wordsworth's phrase, "similitude in dissimilitude" as the verb "die" is repeated but with its tense dramatically altered. A very different epitaph from the 1914–18 war moves the reader by a similar change of tense: "The Devonshires held this trench: they hold it still." There is an effective shift of tenses between the two stanzas of Wordsworth's "A slumber did my spirit seal," and Mackail quotes the final two lines of the poem,

> Rolled round in earth's diurnal course,
> With rocks, and stones, and trees

in order to suggest the art and quality of many Greek epitaphs. He is a little uneasy with their total simplicity and transparency of statement and with the questions such simplicity raises; on two Greek epitaphs, each only two lines long, he writes:

So touching in their stately reserve, so piercing in their delicate austerity, these epitaphs are in a sense the perfection of literature, and yet in another sense almost lie outside its limits.[26]

Of another group of short epitaphs he declares that "Beyond this point simplicity and pathos cannot go"; then he finds that they can, and that no greater depth of pathos can be reached than in "the two simple words *Bene merenti* on a hundred Roman tombs".

But here we have, indeed, moved outside the limits of art; the pathos now is in the situation, and the situation is so poignant that it can (almost) exist without words, or with words as the merest arrows to point to the situation. Perhaps every epitaph tends towards silence; but the urge to silence is countered by the urge to articulate the silence of death, of sorrow and of the grave. From this tension will come those finest epitaphs which satisfy at once the demands of art and the demands of sincerity because they do not recognise the distinction. Wordsworth, as we have seen, was not always certain that the urge to silence ought to be countered, or that words, even as merest arrows, were not too many and too much.

In "The Brothers"[27] (written in 1800 and published the same year in the second edition of *Lyrical Ballads*) Wordsworth tells of two orphan brothers of Ennerdale who had been brought up by their grandfather. The brothers were "the darlings of each other" and when their grandfather died, Leonard, the elder brother

> . . . chiefly for his Brother's sake
> Resolved to try his fortune on the seas.

After twenty years at sea and twelve years without news of him reaching Ennerdale, Leonard, having acquired "some small wealth", decided to return home. The poem opens with Leonard anxiously, but in vain, searching the churchyard for any gravestone that might tell him of his younger brother's death. 'In vain' because, as the priest of Ennerdale says,

> In our church-yard
> Is neither epitaph nor monument,

Tombstone nor name, – only the turf we tread
And a few natural graves.

Leonard complains that such absences seem

> To say that you are heedless of the past:
> An orphan could not find his mother's grave:
> Here's neither head nor foot-stone, place of brass,
> Cross-bones nor skull, – type of our earthly state
> No emblem of our hopes: the dead man's home
> Is but a fellow to that pasture-field.

But the priest replies that

> We have no need of names and epitaphs;
> We talk about the dead by our fire-sides.
> And then, for our immortal part! *we* want
> No symbols, Sir, to tell us that plain tale . . .

It might seem that the "natural graves", the silence of the wordless, uncommemorated green mounds, are beyond the limits ("No symbols, Sir") of art. But even here Wordsworth does not abandon words; it is not true that "the memory of those who are gone seems to continue unaided in the present".[28] "We talk about the dead by our fire-sides"; their memory is kept alive by the talk (the language really used by men but unrecorded by Wordsworth) and the talk is their epitaph.

4

The most moving epitaph for Wordsworth was the nearly wordless child's gravestone. The fact that a woman died of cancer can a little offset the "outrageous expression" of it. Four lines of jingle, Wordsworth says, do not impede the communication of a profound hope in the resurrection. Yet Crabbe's pictures are matters of fact with which the Muses have nothing to do, for the most needful thing in an epitaph is to give to received truths "a spirit which shall re-admit them into the soul like revelations of the moment". In one particular epitaph where the facts themselves might deeply move us, the truth and sincerity come, nevertheless, from the language in which the facts are expressed. Words are mere pointers to a situation, or simply recall to the reader his primary sensations and invite him to "depend upon his feeling, his imagination and his understanding" to turn dross into gold; the Midas touch is not in the words. Yet words are "an incarnation of thought" and not a clothing of it.

We can begin to see the reconciliation of these opposite views on the importance and nature of language by looking at Wordsworth's comments on an epitaph, dated 1673, which he found in a churchyard in Westmorland:

> Under this Stone, Reader, inter'd doth lye,
> 　Beauty and virtue's true epitomy.
> At her appearance the noone-son
> 　Blush'd and shrunk in 'cause quite outdon.
> In her concenter'd did all graces dwell:
> 　God pluck'd my rose that he might take a smel.
> I'll say no more: But weeping wish I may
> 　Soone with thy dear chaste ashes com to lay
> 　　　　　　Sic efflevit Maritus

Can anything go beyond this in extravagance? Yet, if the fundamental thoughts be translated into a natural style, they will be found reasonable and affecting – "The Woman who lies here interred, was in my eyes a perfect image of beauty and virtue; she was to me a brighter object than the Sun in heaven: God took her, who was my delight, from this earth to bring her nearer to himself. Nothing further is worthy to be said than that weeping I wish soon to lie by thy dear chaste ashes – Thus did the Husband pour out his tears" (*Prose Works*, ii, p. 73)

Wordsworth is certain that the writer "notwithstanding his extravagant expression was a sincere mourner". He is certain because he finds in the epitaph an "undercurrent" or "skeleton" of thought and feeling; yet the thought and feeling (the poetry) are not in the words, but in spite of the words; they are in the cruel facts, are, indeed, in the skeleton, the dead body of his wife and in the fact of his grief for her. The "fantastic images" of the writer "though they stain the writing, stained not his soul":

> This simple-hearted Man must have been betrayed by a common notion that what was natural in prose would be out of place in verse; – that it is not the Muse which puts on the Garb but the Garb which makes the Muse. (*Prose Works*, ii, p. 74)

The last words are a little obscure or misleading. Wordsworth seems to be saying that the poem is not in the words but somehow anterior to the words; language is here a clothing of an already existing poem. But elsewhere in the *Essays*, as we have seen, Wordsworth insists that words are not a clothing of thought but an incarnation of it.

In this epitaph the author "wandered from nature in his language". Wordsworth's prose translation, then, will be a return to what he calls a "natural style", a return to nature, indeed, but (Pope's phrase is inevitable) to "nature methodized". Wordsworth's "natural style" turns out to be prose of a regularly formal kind. The "illustrated imagery" has been greatly pruned, and the words, without any vanity of language, draw the reader's attention to the facts of death and grief. In the four lines of jingle, "At the Last day I'm sure I shall appear", etc., which gained Wordsworth's approval, we have to go behind the language to find the feeling; for the words, by their incompetence, draw attention only to themselves and cannot give to the truths which they stumblingly suggest "a pathos and a spirit which shall re-admit them into the soul like the revelations of the moment". Wordsworth's prose translation is, by contrast, transparent. His words "hold a dominion over thoughts" and do not depend for their success on the pathos of the facts, or call upon the reader's "primary sensations" or his already existing feelings or imagination to give them life. On the contrary, his words restore our feelings, reactivate our imaginations; and in the sentence,

"Nothing further is worthy to be said than that weeping I wish soon to lie by thy dear chaste ashes", the line of monosyllables and the dying fall ("the expression and connection of the thoughts") establish the "superior truth and sanctity" of Wordsworth's rewriting of the epitaph. "At the Last day I'm sure I shall appear", etc., may be very close to the language really used by men, but as lines of verse they are anti-literary, and Wordsworth's mistaken endorsement of them is an attack on language itself. His prose epitaph is very different; in its controlled bareness and simplicity the language moves more and more closely to the very facts themselves and, at least in one sentence, the words are converted into "substantial realities" and language becomes the incarnation of thought. In a comment on two lines in Montrose's epitaph,

> I'd weep the world to such a strain,
> As it should deluge once again.

Wordsworth says that the poet's

> soul labours; – the most tremendous event in the history of the Planet, namely, the Deluge, is brought before his imagination by the physical image of tears, – a connection awful from its very remoteness and from the slender bond that unites the ideas. (*Prose Works*, ii, p. 71)

A metaphysical conceit can forge sincerity; and yet, as we saw, it is not the conceit or image ("a mean instrument") but the anterior sincerity of the "afflicted soul" which makes the conceit a mighty vehicle of sincerity. This circular argument is never (cannot ever be) made straight. Wordsworth objects that conceits or "illustrative imagery" are dangerous in epitaphs because they deflect writer and reader from the sanctity of the fact. But, in spite of sudden zig-zags and brief shifts of emphasis in the argument, the *Essays upon Epitaphs* make plain that safety and sincerity will not be found in silence. The great facts which are the staple of all epitaphs – birth, death, grief and hope, the "sensations which all men have felt" – are "truths whose very interest and importance have caused them to be unattended to, as things which could take care of themselves". But these facts and sensations must be given to us by the writer "with the freshness and clearness of an original intuition"; they must, through words, be given flesh if they are to dwell among us. Sincerity will not be most apparent in the honest jingles or stammering ejaculations of a grief-stricken parent. "I know not", says Wordsworth at the end of the third *Essay*, "how I can withdraw more satisfactorily from this long disquisition than by offering to the Reader as a farewell memorial the following Verses, suggested to me by a concise Epitaph which I met with some time ago . . ." The rest is not silence, but a ninety-line extract from *The Excursion*.

The *Essays upon Epitaphs* literally lead us to Wordsworth's own poetic practice – that is their importance – and they define and describe Wordsworth's most characteristic mode of utterance. "Why was not this simply expressed?" Wordsworth demands of an ornate epitaph:

> But alas! ages must pass away before men will have their eyes open to the beauty and majesty of Truth, and will be taught to venerate Poetry no further than as She is a Handmaid pure as her Mistress – the noblest Handmaid in her train! (*Prose Works*, ii, p. 79)

That characteristic mode is a sophisticated simplicity, "a technique of moving restraint"[29] which can through its art enable men to see the fact, "the majesty of Truth". It is a mode which is "matter of fact in its intensity", the mode of understatement. But understatement is still statement; it is statement tending towards silence, but it is in the merely "tending towards" that we find the characteristically Wordsworthian point of balance and reconcilement of opposites. It is not an anti-literary mode (understatement is a device of rhetoric) although Wordsworth paradoxically attempted poems, or parts of poems, in such a mode. F. W. Bateson says that "A certain roughness

about the edges – what Tennyson called the *thick-ankled* element
in Wordsworth's verse – does not seriously affect the quality of his
most characteristic work".[30] There is, of course, such an element
in many poems (usually very early ones) such as "The Thorn",
"The Complaint of a Forsaken Indian Woman", "Goody Blake
and Harry Gill", "We Are Seven"; but if such an element "does
not seriously affect the quality of his most characteristic work" it
is because it is scarcely to be found in such work at all. There is
nothing *thick-ankled* (anti-literary) in "Michael" or "The Ruined
Cottage" or "Resolution and Independence" or *The Prelude*. In
the "Lucy" poems (if we take them in their usual sequence)
Wordsworth moves steadily away from an anti-literary mode to a
more characteristic simplicity. In the first of them, "Strange fits
of passion have I known", she is domesticated and has, very
literally, a local habitation (she lives in a cottage) and a name
(Lucy). In the second, "She dwelt among the untrodden ways",
the details of where and how she lived are less precise; it is the fact
of her importance to the poet which is the heart of the poem. In
the last one, "A slumber did my spirit seal" we learn nothing
about her; she has no name:

> A slumber did my spirit seal;
>   I had no human fears:
> She seemed a thing that could not feel
>   The touch of earthly years.
>
> No motion has she now, no force;
>   She neither hears nor sees;
> Rolled round in earth's diurnal course,
>   With rocks, and stones, and trees.

All that we know about her is that she once lived; but the lines
bring home to us the scandalous *fact* that she whom the writer
loved is now dead, so that we feel "he has mounted to the sources
of things" and reached "the very heart of loss". In this poem
Wordsworth has abandoned those exclamations or "naked
ejaculations" of the earlier ones, " 'Oh Mercy!' to myself I cried"
and ". . . . oh, The difference to me!" where the words only

point to the situation and live off the emotional capital amassed by the earlier lines of the poem. Instead the words now point nowhere; they are no longer arrows but are converted into "substantial realities"; they are no longer "symbols of the passion", but are (in Wordsworth's words) "*things*, active and efficient, which are of themselves part of the passion"[31] which is here a monotonous, sickening, total desolation.

For Roger Sharrock "The Thorn" and other poems are "attempts to get behind poetry altogether . . . they try to overcome in words the brutal limitations of language with its inexorable associations and ambiguities". The notorious lines (altered after 1815)

> I've measured it from side to side;
> 'Tis three feet long and two feet wide.

are merely an extreme case of words as pointers, as merely denotative. As Professor Sharrock says, such things are "absurdities rather than failures".[32] Of a similar stanza in "Simon Lee",

> Few months of life has he in store
> As he to you will tell,
> For still, the more he works, the more
> Do his weak ankles swell,

John F. Danby says that "We are no longer listening to words as literature; we are listening to literature only as it can use words to present the significant facts."[33] An anti-literary use of language can give us significant facts but cannot give us their significance. Professor Danby's comment is true of the lines he quotes, but the complicated rhetoric of "Simon Lee" as a whole stops it from being silly or anti-literary or an assault on language.

But Wordsworth's finest and most typical work is elsewhere, in "Michael" or the "The Ruined Cottage", for example. In "Michael" Isabel knows how much her son's departure will distress his father:

But Isabel was glad when Sunday came
To stop her in her work: for, when she lay
By Michael's side, she through the last two nights
Heard him, how he was troubled in his sleep:
And when they rose at morning she could see
That all his hopes were gone. That day at noon
She said to Luke, while they two by themselves
Were sitting at the door, "Thou must not go:
We have no other Child but thee to lose,
None to remember – do not go away,
For if thou leave thy Father he will die."

Michael takes his son to the heap of stones with which he had hoped to build a sheep-fold:

"This was a work for us; and now, my Son,
It is a work for me."

He asks Luke, before they leave, to lay the corner-stone:

"Now, fare thee well –
When thou return'st, thou in this place wilt see
A work which is not here: a covenant
'Twill be between us; but, whatever fate
Befall thee, I shall love thee to the last,
And bear thy memory with me to the grave."

The Shepherd ended here; and Luke stooped down,
And, as his Father had requested, laid
The first stone of the Sheep-fold. At the sight
The old Man's grief broke from him; to his heart
He pressed his Son, he kissed him and wept;
And to the house together they returned.

In "The Ruined Cottage" Margaret tells of her growing fear that her husband will not return:

"I have slept
Weeping, and weeping have I waked; my tears

Have flowed as if my body were not such
As others are; and I could never die."

These few, brief extracts tell of moving and pathetic situations;
but (Wordsworth's question is apt) "who does not here feel a
superior truth and sincerity, which is not dependent upon the
circumstances, but merely the result of the expression and
connection of the thoughts?" An uncompleted sheep-fold will
suggest sad thoughts; the poem itself incarnates them. Michael's
words fail him at last; he weeps and falls silent. Wordsworth's
words do not fail him, and he does not go silent. The proposed
"covenant" (the sheep-fold) becomes in the end an epitaph, but
an epitaph of an anti-literary kind, an uncompleted circle of
stones which can exist without words, a silent poem. The poem
itself is an epitaph of a different kind, a completed circle of words
with the monosyllables assembled like stones and made into
"substantial realities". Calling such words "a selection of the
language really used by men", no matter what the circumstances, does nothing to define a poetic mode of "moving
restraint". It is not selection, however defined, that we aware of,
but those additions ("borrowing sometimes a Bible turn of
expression") which Wordsworth admitted could be a part of
selection. The biblical borrowings are sometimes words ("covenant", "troubled") as well as turns of expression. One such
(literal) turn of expression is "I have slept/Weeping, and
weeping have I waked", which in the formality of its inversions
and circular shape enacts, incarnates the day and night cycle of
Margaret's despair. "I do not know", said Wordsworth in the
Preface to *Lyrical Ballads*, "how to give my Reader a more exact
notion of the style in which it was my wish and intention to write,
than by informing him that I have at all times endeavoured to
look steadily at my subject."[34] It is in this looking (done "through
the steady light of words"[35]) in this Wordsworthian act of
attention until the thing looked at becomes the word itself
("words are *powers* either to kill or animate") that the morality
(sincerity) and poetry of the poem as epitaph are to be found.

3 "The Streaks of the Tulip"

> The business of a poet . . . is to examine, not the individual, but the species; to remark general properties and large appearances: he does not number the streaks of the tulip
>
> Johnson, *Rasselas*

Jeffrey, as we saw, was scornful of "Strange fits of passion have I known" and particularly of the two last lines:

> "O mercy!" to myself I cried,
> "If Lucy should be dead"

He was prepared to leave it to "any reader of common candour and discernment" – the common reader – to say

> whether these representations of character and sentiment are drawn from that eternal and universal standard of truth and nature, which every one is knowing enough to recognize, and no one great enough to depart from with impunity; or whether they are not formed, as we have ventured to allege, upon certain fantastic and affected peculiarities in the mind or fancy of the author . . .

He goes on to accuse Wordsworth of "wide and wilful aberrations from ordinary nature" and turns against him "the author's own admission of the narrowness of the plan upon which he writes".[1] Jeffrey is reasserting the neo-classic theory that it is the job of the poet to imitate nature (by this is usually meant human nature) which is everywhere the same. He must not deal with the particular, for this easily becomes the odd (fit subject for the grotesque) or that "fantastic and affected" peculiarity which the eighteenth century called "singularity". Jeffrey's comments would have surprised and would not have surprised Wordsworth. They would have surprised him because he always claimed to be supporting Jeffrey's "universal standard of truth and nature"; they would not have surprised him since he did not expect Jeffrey to appreciate those "more subtle windings" of ordinary human nature which Wordsworth wished to trace.

Wordsworth's neo-classic vocabulary conceals subtle, important shifts of meaning and value. Even in early letters a traditional critical position is being used for radical purposes. In a letter to Coleridge in 1799 Wordsworth says that poetry should present "manners":

> not transitory manners reflecting the wearisome unintelligible obliquities of city-life, but manners connected with the permanent objects of nature and partaking of the simplicity of those objects. Such pictures must interest when the original shall cease to exist. The reason will be immediately obvious if you consider yourself as lying in a valley on the side of mount Etna reading one of Theocritus's Idylliums or on the plains of Attica with a comedy of Aristophanes on your hand. Of Theocritus and his spirit perhaps three fourths remain of Aristophanes a mutilated skeleton . . . read Theocritus in Ayrshire of Merionethshire and you will find perpetual occasions to recollect what you see daily in Ayrshire or Merionelhshire, read Congreve Vanbrugh and Farquhar in London and though not a century is elapsed since they were alive and merry, you will meet with whole pages that are uninteresting and incomprehensive (*EY*, p. 255)

Human nature is uniform, as Dr Johnson would agree, but it seems that it is more uniform in some places than in others. It is not enough to agree with Johnson that the poet must "trace the changes of the human mind as they are modified by various institutions and accidental influences of climate or custom";[2]

human nature cannot properly be studied in cities, since in cities no stability of the human mind is possible, and therefore the permanent forms of human nature can be properly studied only in the country among men in "humble and rustic life". Wordsworth goes on to praise Burns because in his work "you have manners everywhere". There is no individual character in all Burns's poems ("Tam Shanter I do not deem a character") except his own. "But every where you have the presence of human life" (that is, general human nature); "the communications that proceed from Burns come to the mind with the life and charm of recognitions".

The neo-classicist sees human nature as constant and sees that men "however distinguished by external accidents or intrinsick qualities have all the same wants, the same pains, and, as far as the senses are consulted, the same pleasures". This constancy moved Johnson to memorable statement:

> We are all prompted by the same motives, all deceived by the same fallacies, all animated by hope, obstructed by danger, entangled by desire, and seduced by pleasure.

In his letter to Coleridge, Wordsworth was less generously inclusive than the great Tory.

> We are all naked till we are dressed, and hungry till we are fed; and the general's triumph, and sage's disputation, end, like the humble labours of the smith or plowman, in a dinner or in sleep.

Even when he is not meditating so deliberately on the vanity of human wishes, Johnson can find "amidst all the disorder and inequality" which variety of life and occupation and training produces in men, "such a general and remote similitude, as may be expected in the same common nature affected by external circumstances indefinitely varied". For Johnson the poet is the same as anybody else:

Writers of all ages have had the same sentiments, because they have in all ages had the same objects of speculation; the interests and passions, the virtues and vices of mankind, have been diversified in different times, only by unessential and casual varieties.[3]

The poet is very simply a man speaking to men, and he will speak to them of those sentiments which they can equally discover in themselves and "in minds distant a thousand years from one another". It is because there is "a general similitude that goes through the whole race of mankind" that Sir Joshua Reynolds says it is possible to establish the rules of art; because human nature is uniform, "What has pleased, and continues to please, is likely to please again: hence are derived the rules of art, and on this immovable foundation they must ever stand . . ."[4] The poet's responsibility is to stress this "general similitude" since, as Johnson says, "Nothing can please many, and please long, but just representations of general nature".[5]

How can we discover what general nature is, so that we may judge the success of a writer in describing it? Since the proper study of mankind is man, we can either

> Let Observation with extensive View
> Survey Mankind from *China* to Peru;

or we can come at the truth by introspection ("Know then thyself"), by examining (in Reynolds's phrase) "what passes in our own bosoms". "In fact, as he who does not know himself, does not know others, so may it be said with equal truth that he who does not know others, knows himself but very imperfectly." Since we can suppose a uniformity in all men, such self-inspection will enable us to conclude "that the same effect will be produced by the same cause in the minds of others",[6] and therefore to agree with Pope that "whatever is very good sense must have been common sense in all times". There may well be, admits Dr Johnson, an occasional "anomalous mind" which does not feel like others (an Idiot Boy or old Cumberland Beggar?) but every man "carries the archetype within him" of those human passions which it is the business of the writer to describe. It is thus that we can recognise Shakespeare as the greatest neo-classic writer; he is, says Johnson, above all others "the poet of nature; the poet that holds up to his readers a faithful mirror of manners and of life". Wordsworth praised Burns because in his work there were "manners everywhere"; Shakespeare's characters are not modified by the customs of particular places, but are

> the genuine progeny of common humanity, such as the world will always supply, and observation will always find. His persons act and speak by the influence of those general passions and principles by which all minds are agitated. . . . In the writings of other poets a character is too often an individual; in those of Shakespeare it is commonly a species.[7]

Johnson admires in Shakespeare what Wordsworth admires in Burns, "the presence of human life" and the absence of individual character. Burns and Shakespeare hold the mirror up to nature but not to what Reynolds calls "accidental deviations from her accustomed practice"; for only the "general idea therefore ought to be called nature; and nothing else, correctly speaking, has a right to that name". We are wrong, Reynolds explains, to call Rembrandt's "exact representations of individual objects" nature:

> This misapplication of terms must be very often perplexing to the young student. Is not art, he may say, an imitation of nature? Must he not, therefore, who imitated her with the greatest fidelity, be the best artist? By this mode of reasoning Rembrandt has a higher place than Raffaelle. But a very little reflection will serve to show us, that these particularities cannot be nature: for how can that be the nature of man, in which no two individuals are the same?

Reynolds equates nature with "universal opinion". His "particularities" easily become Johnson's "peculiarities", and so we arrive at that "singularity" which is, says Johnson, "I think, in its own nature universally and invariably displeasing". In Reynolds and Johnson moral and literary (or artistic) criticism are not kept apart. "We are perpetually moralists," said Johnson, "but we are geometricians only by chance", and for "geometrician" we can read "writer" or "critic". Singularity in man is a moral fault, and the writer who deals with such "deformity" is equally condemned; in both cases it is a mark of pride. A man, says Reynolds, who resists the authority of others "leaves open every argument to singularity, vanity, self-conceit, obstinacy and many other vices". Our submission to others, whether as men or artists, "is a deference which we owe" for we can never be satisfied with our opinions "till they are ratified and confirmed by the suffrages of the rest of mankind". Johnson's quarrel with the metaphysical poets was a profoundly moral one: their conceit led them to attempt the unexpected and surprising, and so to disregard "that uniformity of sentiment which enables us to conceive and to excite the pains and pleasures of other minds". Because their thoughts were often new they were seldom natural or just. "Their wish was only to say what they hoped had never been said before"; and because they "lay on the watch for novelty" they could not hope for greatness, for "great thoughts are always general and consist in positions not limited by exceptions", and "great things cannot have escaped former observation".[8]

In the *Essay, Supplementary to the Preface* (1815) Wordsworth speaks of the need to divest "the reader of the pride that induces him to dwell upon those points wherein men differ from each other, to the exclusion of those in which all men are the same".[9] But Wordsworth's dilemma and his need to extend the scope of neo-classic vocabulary and views on general nature and general truth are suggested in some words of Dr Johnson's which prophetically describe Wordsworth's critical reception:

All violation of established practice, implies in its own nature a rejection of the common opinion, a defiance of common censure, and an appeal from general laws to private judgement; he, therefore, who differs from others without apparent advantage, ought not to be angry if his arrogance is punished with ridicule; if those, whose example he superciliously overlooks, point him out to derision, and hoot him back again into the common road.[10]

This reads like a hostile early criticism of *Lyrical Ballads*; yet Wordsworth did not want to reject common opinion; he wanted to reform it. He did not wish to appeal from general laws to private judgement, but wanted to reveal general laws of which his readers might be ignorant, and to reveal them, perhaps, in unlikely places.

The Advertisement to *Lyrical Ballads* states simply that the materials of poetry are to be found "in every subject which can interest the human mind". Readers of "our elder writers" will not be dismayed by any familiarity in expression, but will see that the writer has successfully painted "manners and passions". The emphasis alters slightly in the first edition of the Preface; but it is in the additions and changes of 1802 that Wordsworth's neo-classical language begins to bend under the strain of the enlarged meanings being imposed upon it. In 1800, "The principal object . . . . which I proposed to myself in these Poems was to make the incidents of common life interesting by tracing in them, truly though not ostentatiously, the primary laws of our nature." In 1802 the poetic function is more obvious; "tracing" is replaced by "describing"; the modest "truly though not ostentatiously" (which is close to Johnson's "deliberately but not dogmatically") is boosted by the wish to throw over these primary (that is, general) laws of our nature "a certain colouring of imagination, whereby ordinary things should be presented to the mind in an unusual aspect".[11] (An aspect, of course, might become so unusual as to constitute "singularity".)

The main shift of the 1800 Preface, as I suggested in the first chapter, is to make the reader share with the poet responsibility for the success of the poem. The "primary laws of our nature" will be the subject of his poems, but only a reader "in a healthful state of association" will be able to see that what the poet describes really *are* primary laws and not eccentricities. The purpose of his poems is "to follow the fluxes and refluxes of the mind when agitated by the great and simple affections of our nature". This is close to Dr Johnson's reminder that the poet must have "regard to that uniformity of sentiment which enables us to conceive and to excite the pains and pleasures of other minds";[12] but Wordsworth immediately warns the reader that in "The Idiot Boy" and "The Mad Mother", the maternal passion "will be traced through many of its more subtle windings". The notion of normal or general human nature is obviously being extended, and we are beginning to look for it where we should not have expected to find it. In "Simon Lee" Wordsworth is "placing my Reader in the way of receiving from ordinary moral sensations another and more salutory impression than we are accustomed to receive from them". We are merely being "placed" in the way of receiving such impressions and so of being "in some degree enlightened": the pearls have been cast before us; it will depend on our "healthful state of association" whether we gather them or not. A few lines later Wordsworth offers "Old Man Travelling" and "The Two Thieves" for the reader's approval since the characters in these poems are made up of simple elements, "such as exist now and will probably always exist". At this point Wordsworth seems to alter the usual neo-classic meaning of "manners". The old man and the thieves, he says, belong "rather to nature than to manners". For Johnson and Fielding there is no opposition: nature *is* manners ("I describe not men, but manners; not an individual but a species"). Wordsworth is forced to oppose the terms since his aims in "Old Man Travelling" could not be comprehended by any normal usage of eighteenth-century critical vocabulary.[13]

In a letter of 1801 to Charles James Fox, Wordsworth says that the poems in *Lyrical Ballads* (He is referring particularly to "The Brothers" and "Michael") "are faithful copies from nature", but the reader still has responsibilities which he may be unable or unwilling to shoulder:

I hope, whatever effect they may have upon you, you will at least be able to perceive that they may excite profitable sympathies in many kind and good hearts, and may in some small degree enlarge . . . our knowledge of human nature, by shewing that our best qualities are possessed by men whom we are too apt to consider, not with reference to the points in which they resemble us, but to those in which they manifestly differ from us. (*EY*, p. 315)

Wordsworth suggests that an extension of the usual subjects of poetry to include, for example, an old Cumberland shepherd, may make the poet more truly neo-classic, more extensively and thoroughly concerned with the proper study of mankind, Man. In the 1800 Preface he speaks of "qualities of the human mind". The phrase is important if we remember Wordsworth's sharp insistence on the difference between the definite and indefinite article; a reader was once rebuked for referring to the " 'poem on a Daisy' (by the bye, it is on *the* Daisy, a mighty difference)". "The great and universal passions of men" constitute "the most valuable object in all writing whether in prose or verse", and "Goody Blake and Harry Gill", which is "one of the rudest of this collection", illustrates one such passion – that the power of imagination can produce changes "even in our physical nature". Wordsworth's poem is at once general and particular: "The truth is an important one; the fact (for it is a *fact*) is a valuable illustration of it."

Wordsworth is afraid that he may have been sometimes too particular:

I am sensible that my associations must have sometimes been particular instead of general, and that, consequently, giving to things a false importance, sometimes from diseased impulses I may have written upon unworthy subjects . . . (*Prose Works*, i, p. 152)

He may not have risen sufficiently above what Sir Joshua Reynolds deplored as "singular forms, local customs, particularities, and details of every kind". But only *may* have written;

Wordsworth is reluctant to accept the reader's objections (Reynolds insisted that the "well-disciplined mind . . . submits its own opinion to the public voice") since "the Reader ought never to forget that he is himself exposed to the same errors as the Poet", and, indeed, more likely to judge wrongly than the poet; for "since he is so much less interested in the subject, he may decide lightly and carelessly".[14] Wordsworth's uneasiness comes from a different and loftier notion of what a poet should be and from a decline of confidence in the modern poet's audience. In the 1802 edition of the Preface unease becomes strain as Wordsworth, while insisting that a poet is a man speaking to men, makes passionately clear his belief in the poet's difference from other men and his superiority to them. The poet now has "more enthusiasm" than other men, "a greater knowledge of human nature, and a more comprehensive soul than are supposed to be common among mankind".

The year 1802 is the high-water mark of Wordsworth's dissatisfaction (and not simply in the revised Preface) with neo-classic theories of general human nature and with the belief that these alone are the fit subject of poetry. But dissatisfaction is not rejection; Wordsworth adds to the 1800 Preface (most famously the "What is a Poet" passage) but he does not subtract from it. Thus the 1802 Preface provides us in some ways with two documents, as Wordsworth tries unsuccessfully to adopt and then adapt an outworn critical terminology (with the assumptions it carries) to his own more private and revolutionary purposes. It is, once again, new wine in old bottles; the remarkable thing is Wordsworth's attachment to these old bottles. In one of the 1802 additions he writes that Poetry is "the image of man and nature". (The phrase could be Johnson's.) And since a poet must delight by instructing, he

> writes under one restriction only, namely, the necessity of giving immediate pleasure to a human Being possessed of that information which may be expected from him, not as a lawyer, a physician, a mariner, an astronomer, or a natural philosopher, but as a Man. (*Prose Works*, i, p. 139)

The neo-classic generosity is barely visible in the qualifications. Which human beings? How many are possessed of this necessary information? And what is this information which can be expected of them? The questions scarcely arose for Johnson "since there are many occasions in which all reasonable men will nearly think alike"; but they arise for Wordsworth, and in a letter of the same year to Professor Wilson ("Christopher North") he suggests some possible answers. To Wilson's complaint of "The Idiot Boy" that nothing is a fit subject for poetry which does not please, Wordsworth replies: "But here follows a question, Does not please whom?" The answer is "human nature, as it has been and ever will be". Where are we to find "the best measure" of human nature?

> I answer, from within; by stripping our own hearts naked, and by looking out of ourselves towards men who lead the simplest lives most according to nature men who have never known false refinements . . . artificial desires . . . effeminate habits of thinking and feeling . . . People in our rank of life, are perpetually falling into one sad mistake, namely, that of supposing that human nature and the persons they associate with are one and the same thing. Whom do we generally associate with? Gentlemen, persons of fortune, professional men, ladies persons . . . These persons are, it is true, a part of human nature, but we err lamentably if we suppose them to be fair representatives of the vast mass of human existence.

It is not enough that Wilson praises him for faithfully reflecting in his poems "the feelings of human nature":

> I would fain hope that I had done so. But a great Poet ought to do more than this; he ought to a certain degree to rectify men's feelings, to give them new compositions of feeling, to render their feelings more sane pure and permanent, in short, more consonant to nature, that is, to eternal nature, and the great moving spirit of things. He ought to travel before men occasionally as well as at their sides.

As an example Wordsworth refers to "The Idiot Boy" and declares that

> the loathing and disgust which many people have at the sight of an Idiot, is a feeling which, though having some foundation in human nature is not necessarily attached to it in any [virtuous?] degree, but is owing, in a great measure to a false delicacy, and . . . a certain want of comprehensiveness of thinking and feeling. Persons in the lower classes of society have little or nothing of this . . . . Poor people . . . easily forget whatever there is of natural disgust about them . . . They are worshipped . . . in several parts of the East. Among the Alps where they are numerous, they are considered, I believe, as a blessing to the family to which they belong. (*EY*, pp. 354–7)

In other words, we must be really much more ruthless in our introspection ("by stripping our hearts naked") and more thorough in our survey of mankind from China to Peru (not forgetting to take in on our way the remoter dales of Cumberland) before we make confident definitions of general human nature. If some readers make the mistake of supposing that "human nature and the persons they associate with are one and the same thing", this suggests that place and circumstance can so shape people that any inclusive attempt to define general human nature will be (at the least) very difficult. Wordsworth's reluctant dismissive concession, "These persons are, it is true, a part of human nature", makes his dilemma more obvious. How have such educated readers nearly outlawed themselves? The letter suggests only by "false refinements" and "artificial desires"; but it offers a likely remedy: such readers "must descend lower among cottages and fields and among children. A man must have done this habitually before his judgment upon the Idiot Boy would be in any way decisive with me." That is, go and study human nature where it may best be found. The opposition is between town and country; "false refinements" and "artificial desires" are more likely to be found in the town, and since more

and more people are living in towns ("the increasing accumu-
lation of men in cities") men are becoming less obviously
representatives of general and unchanging human nature; a
"multitude of causes" are reducing men's minds "to a state of
almost savage torpor".

There is here a faint fear that the very idea of a general human
nature which does not change from place to place or year to year
is threatened, a prophetic fear of the coming historicism. At
almost the same time Walter Scott shows a similar uncertainty.
In the first chapter of *Waverley* (a chapter probably written in
1805) Scott refers to "those passions common to men in all stages
of society" and which have "agitated the human heart" from the
fifteenth century to the present day:

> Upon these passions it is no doubt true that the state of
> manners and laws casts a necessary colouring; but the
> bearings, to use the language of heraldry, remain the same,
> though the tincture may be not only different, but opposed in
> strong contradistinction.

By 1819 the uncertainty implied by the last four words was more
marked. In the Dedicatory Epistle to *Ivanhoe* "the passions" are
"generally the same in all ranks and conditions, all countries and
ages". "Our ancestors were not more distinct from us, surely,
than Jews are from Christians" and the "tenor of their affections
and feelings must have borne the same general proportion to our
own." Words like "surely" and "must have" are signs of Scott's
unease.

Wordsworth's fear is the merest hint and he never returned to
it. His more impressive response is a radical-conservative one; he
takes neo-classic principles more seriously than they were ever
taken, and by extending their scope he breathes new life into
them. Reynolds writes in his "Fifth Discourse":

> The works, whether of poets, painters, moralists, or historians,
> which are built upon general nature, live for ever; while those

which depend for their existence on particular customs and habits, a partial view of nature, or the fluctuation of fashion, can be coeval with that which first raised them from obscurity. Present time and future may be considered as rivals, and he who solicits the one must expect to be discountenanced by the other.

Some of the phrases here, "partial view", "fluctuation of fashion", are very close to the objections which Wordsworth makes in his letter to Professor Wilson; for Wordsworth, as for Reynolds, works must be built upon general nature if they are to live for ever. In which case let us get rid of "partial views" (Wordsworth finds them chiefly in city-dwellers) and search for those feelings which are "permanent" and which are really "more consonant to . . . eternal nature".

Is Wordsworth leading a revolution, or is he *plus royaliste que le roi*? Does it amount to the same thing? His conservative phraseology and his apparent wish merely to extend neo-classic theory are, whether intentionally or not, a cover for more insidious intentions. His aim is to restore human nature and to make men more truly and deeply representative of general human nature. "It is not enough for me as a poet, to delineate merely such feelings as all men *do* sympathise with but, it is also highly desirable to add to these others, such as all men may sympathise with . . ."[15] He can show men where to find this truer human nature (chiefly among country people) and, by bringing it before men's eyes in poems, can extend their knowledge of it. He can do this because, as a poet, he "has a greater knowledge of human nature". The poet, indeed, now seems to be the supreme example of general human nature; he has the ability to conjure up in himself passions which "more nearly resemble the passions produced by real events, than anything which, from the motions of their own minds merely, other men are accustomed to feel in themselves".[16] But though a supreme example, the poet does not differ "in kind from other men, but only in degree", and the "passions and thoughts and feelings" which he expresses are "the general thoughts and passions and feelings of men":

And with what are they connected? Undoubtedly with our moral sentiments and animal sensations, and with the causes which excite these; with the operations of the elements, and the appearances of the visible universe; with storm and sunshine, with the revolutions of the seasons, with cold and heat, with loss of friends and kindred, with injuries and resentments, gratitude and hope, with fear and sorrow. These, and the like, are the sensations and objects which the Poet describes, as they are the sensations of other men, and the objects which interest them. The Poet thinks and feels in the spirit of human passions. (*Prose Works*, i, p. 142)

This is a generous but imprecise description of general truth. It seems after all (to reverse Wordsworth's phrase), that the poet describes not such feelings as all men *may* sympathise with, but such feelings, as all men *do* sympathise with. It is precisely because of Wordsworth's "sublime notion of Poetry" and his lofty view of the poet, and because the "divine spirit" of the poet can "aid the transfiguration" of all things, that he will be less likely than any other writer to "break in upon the sanctity and truth of his pictures by transitory and accidental ornaments".[17]

In the *Essays upon Epitaphs* Wordsworth moves away from such high views of the poet and poetry and from the ambitious attempt (dependent on such views) to stretch the notions of general human nature and general truth. The very nature of the epitaph compels a more traditional and restricted use of such terms:

We suffer and we weep with the same heart; we love and are anxious for one another in one spirit; our hopes look to the same quarter; and the virtues by which we are all to be furthered and supported, as patience, meekness, good-will, justice, temperance, and temperate desires, are in an equal degree the concern of us all. Let an Epitaph, then, contain at least these acknowledgements of our common Nature . . . (*Prose Works*, ii, p. 59)

An epitaph tells of death and sorrow and hope, sentiments with which, at all times and in all places, all men may sympathise without instruction; it speaks "the general language of humanity as connected with the subject of death . . . and of life. To be born and to die are the two points in which all men feel themselves to be in absolute coincidence".[18] The epitaph, then, reconciles all men through this "absolute coincidence" of general truths which flow from our common human nature. But an epitaph does not simply speak of life and death; it speaks of a particular person who was alive and is now dead and lamented, and it must therefore achieve a reconciliation of general truth with a particular case. An epitaph must deal with the public expression of a private sorrow which all men have known or will one day know. It must concern itself with the physical body buried there in the grave, and with the spirit of the dead man which lives on in the memories of the living and, through the epitaph, in the imaginations of strangers and of those as yet unborn; as Wordsworth's daffodils, though long dead when he wrote the poem, were kept alive in his memory, and through the poem have lived in the imaginations of generations of readers.

It is the special distinction of the epitaph that it can achieve this reconciliation of general and particular. Dr Johnson knew about the problem when he complained that Pope's epitaph "On the Monument of the Hon. Robert Digby, and of his sister Mary" "contains of the brother only a general, indiscriminate character, and of the sister tells us nothing but that she died. The difficulty in writing epitaphs is to give a particular and appropriate praise". At the beginning of the first *Essay* Wordsworth tells a story which acts as a parable of his intention:

Simonides, it is related, upon landing in a strange country, found the corse of an unknown person lying by the sea-side; he buried it, and was honoured throughout Greece for the piety of that act. Another ancient Philosopher, chancing to fix his eyes upon a dead body, regarded the same with slight, if not with contempt; saying, "See the shell of the flown bird!" But it is not to be supposed that the moral and tender-hearted Simonides was incapable of the lofty movements of thought, to which that other Sage gave way . . . And with regard to this latter we may be assured that, if he had been destitute of the capability of communing with the more exalted thoughts that appertain to human nature, he would have cared no more for the corse of the stranger than for the dead body of a seal or porpoise which might have been cast up by the waves. (*Prose Works*, ii, p. 52)

Man has both corporeal frame and immortal soul. Both the philosophers were "in sympathy with the best feelings of our nature; feelings which, though they seem opposite to each other, have another and finer connection than that of contrast". The writer of an epitaph reconciles these different and opposed sentiments; he stands on a "midway point" which "commands the thoughts and feelings of the two Sages whom we have represented in contrast". A sepulchral monument, explains Wordsworth, guards the physical remains of the deceased and keeps alive their memory; it is "a tribute to man as a human being". An epitaph "includes this general feeling" but does more; it is

a record to preserve the memory of the dead, as a tribute to his individual worth, for a satisfaction to the sorrowing hearts of the survivors, and for the common benefit of the living: which record is to be accomplished, not in a general manner, but, where it can, in *close connection with the bodily remains of the deceased* . . . (*Prose Works*, ii, p. 53)

The movement here is that of "The Ruined Cottage" in Book I of *The Excursion* (Wordsworth reprinted the first *Essay* as a note to the poem). The poem preserves the "individual worth" of Margaret for a satisfaction to the survivors, in this case the Wanderer, and for the common benefit of the living, here the poet and all subsequent readers of the tale.

That the epitaph must reconcile particular and general is more clearly stated in the same *Essay*: "The first requisite, then, in an Epitaph is, that it should speak, in a tone which shall sink into the heart, the general language of humanity. . . ." This general language "may be uttered so strikingly as to entitle an epitaph to the highest praise", but it cannot lay claim to the highest unless it has other and different qualities. The "perfection" of an epitaph

> will be found to lie in a due proportion of the common or universal feeling of humanity to sensations excited by a distinct and clear conception, conveyed to the reader's mind, of the individual, whose death is deplored and whose memory is to be preserved; at least of his character as, after death, it appeared to those who loved him and lament his loss. The general sympathy ought to be quickened, provoked, and diversified, by particular thoughts, actions, images, – circumstances of age, occupation, manner of life, prosperity which the deceased had known, or adversity to which he had been subject; and these ought to be bound together and solemnized into one harmony by the general sympathy. The two powers should temper, restrain, and exalt each other. The reader ought to know who and what the man was whom he is called upon to think of with interest. A distinct conception should be given (implicitly where it can, rather than explicitly) of the individual lamented. (*Prose Works*, ii, p. 57)

Phrase after phrase in the passage, such as "general sympathy" and "particular thoughts", stresses the need for synthesis. The "two powers" may for brevity's sake be called the general and the particular. Professor Lindenberger claims that Wordsworth's critical writings "take for granted the traditional distinctions between *pathos* and *ethos*", and that it is more accurate to interpret the above passage as a reconciliation of these two traditional and "opposing types of emotion which poetry seeks to depict". These "two powers" interact to " 'temper' (presumably the influence of *ethos* upon *pathos*), 'exalt' (the influence of *pathos* upon *ethos*), and 'restrain' (perhaps the mutual effect of each upon the other)".[19]

The "two powers" should restrain each other, but ethos, perhaps, needs more restraint than pathos since in an epitaph it is "much better . . . to fall short in discrimination than to pursue it too far, or to labour it unfeelingly". For Dr Johnson, as we saw, "particular praise" would be difficult to supply in an epitaph since "the greater part of mankind *have no character at all*, have little that distinguishes them from others equally good or bad" and therefore nothing distinctive can be said of them. Wordsworth's rejection of too much particular comment is more decorous and humane and more richly neo-classic. Too much detail is inappropriate because "to analyse the characters of others, especially of those whom we love, is not a common or natural employment of men at any time", and least of all when "under the pressure of sorrow, admiration, or regret". By the very circumstances of an epitaph we are in no place "so much disposed to dwell upon those points, of nature and condition, wherein all men resemble each other as . . . by the side of the grave which gathers all human Beings to itself, and 'equalises the lofty and the low' ".[20] Dr Johnson had praised an epitaph of Pope's because it contained "nothing taken from common-places". Wordsworth's answer is firm:

> it is not only no fault but a primary requisite in an Epitaph that it shall contain thoughts and feelings which are in their substance common-place, and even trite. It is grounded upon the universal intellectual property of man; – sensations which all men have felt and feel in some degree daily and hourly; – truths whose very interest and importance have caused them to be unattended to, as things which could take care of themselves. (*Prose Works*, ii, p. 78)

An epitaph, therefore, must contain "these acknowledgements to our common nature", and our "sense of their importance" must not be "sacrificed to a balance of opposite qualities or minute distinctions in individual character". A "balance of opposite qualities", however, is not a reconcilement, but is, in fact, the feature which most damns some of Pope's epitaphs. In his lines on Mrs Corbet Pope has "no other aim than to give a favourable *Portrait* of the character of the deceased". In general the epitaphs of Pope "cannot well be too severely condemned"; they are almost without "those universal feelings and simple movements of mind which we have called for as indispensible". Pope's satiric habits and use of the heroic couplet were against him; his mind had been "employed chiefly in observation upon the vices and follies of men"; that is, upon deviations from the norm instead of the sentiments common to us all. (The writer of satire will inevitably dwell on such deviation or "singularity".) The heroic couplet encouraged balance and antithesis; it is reasonable in Pope's satiric portraits that "the page should be suitably crowded with antithetical expressions", but it is disastrous in his epitaphs where "one half of the process is mechanical, words doing their own work, and one half of the line manufacturing the rest". In these cases "The Author forgets that it is a living creature that must interest us and not an intellectual Existence".[21] Unlike the satirist, the writer of an epitaph composes by "the grave of one whom he loves and admires"; he shrinks "from the thought of placing [his] merits and defects to be weighed against each other in the nice balance of pure intellect"; he is neither "an atomist, who dissects the internal frame of the mind",[22] nor

> . . . a fingering slave
> One that would peep and botanize
> Upon his mother's grave? (*PW*, iv, p. 66)

For Dr Johnson, too, antithetical expressions were scarcely satisfactory, since the total, balanced picture which such expressions aim to supply is not what is needed in an epitaph: "Though a sepulchral inscription is professedly a panegyrick, and, therefore, not confined to historical impartiality, yet it ought always to be written with regard to truth."[23] We are not to tell lies in an epitaph nor attribute qualities to the dead which they did not have; but we ought not to detail their faults or crimes, since an epitaph is "to exhibit patterns of virtue". Johnson and Wordsworth can both agree that what is factually true is not necessarily a part of general truth, but Wordsworth expresses Johnson's point in very different language. The character of a dead person "is not seen, no – nor ought to be seen, otherwise than as a tree through a tender haze or a luminous mist, that spiritualises and beautifies it". Such a haze or mist will conceal and take away things "but only to the end that the parts which are not abstracted may appear more dignified and lovely". But this is still a "faithful image". "It *is* truth, and of the highest order"; for though certain things do not appear which did exist, yet "the object being looked at through this medium, parts and proportions are brought into distinct view which before had been only imperfectly or unconsciously seen". "Laborious and antithetic discriminations" defeat their own purpose and deny the sincerity of an epitaph; "for, the understanding having been so busy in its petty occupation, how could the heart of the mourner be other than cold?" An epitaph is "truth hallowed by love – the joint offspring of the worth of the dead and the affections of the living!"[24] (The reconcilement in these phrases is an example of what Coleridge meant when he talked of Wordsworth's "fine balance of truth in observing, with the imaginative faculty in modifying, the objects observed".)[25]

In an epitaph, then, "what was peculiar to the individual shall still be subordinate to a sense of what he had in common with the species" in order that the epitaph may effectively teach and instruct, by "exhortation and admonition" (Wordsworth's phrase) or, as Dr Johnson says, by example.[26] And this will be true whether the epitaph be long or short. Wordsworth had been moved to write the *Essays* by his admiration for the epitaphs of Chiabrera, and these were sometimes short (like the epitaphs on Tasso or on himself) or much longer ones which Wordsworth insists still remain epitaphs and not elegies. Wordsworth says of his own epitaph on Charles Lamb:

Chiabrera has been here my model . . . His epitaphs are characteristic and circumstantial – so have I endeavoured to make this of mine – but I have not ventured to touch upon the most striking feature of our departed friend's character and the most affecting circumstance of his life, viz. his faithful and intense love of his Sister. Had I been pouring out an Elegy or Monody, this would and must have been done . . . (*PW*, iv, p. 458)

("Characteristic" means "giving the character of".) An elegy does not achieve that exact reconcilement of particular and general which is the mark of an epitaph; the intimate details of Charles Lamb's "faithful and intense" love for his sister are unsuitable because they are so affecting, and because the "too poignant and transitory" is always an unfit subject for an epitaph. Wordsworth had found fault, in his third *Essay*, with a phrase from an epitaph supposedly written by a husband on his dead wife:

> "*Speak! dead Maria breathe a strain divine!*" This verse flows nobly from the heart and the imagination; but perhaps it is not one of those impassioned thoughts which should be fixed in language upon a sepulchral stone. It is in its nature too poignant and transitory. A Husband meditating by his Wife's grave would throw off such a feeling, and would give voice to it; and it would be in its place in a Monody to her Memory but, if I am not mistaken, ought to have been suppressed here, or uttered after a different manner. (*Prose Works*, ii, p. 83)

What should this "different manner" be? Wordsworth had read John Weever's *Ancient Funeral Monuments* . . . (1631)[27] and in the third *Essay* accepts Weever's definition of an epitaph:

> "An Epitaph", says Weever, "is a superscription (either in verse or prose) or an astrict pithie Diagram, writ, carved or engraven, upon the tomb, grave, or sepulchre of the defunct, briefly declaring (*and that with a kind of commiseration*) the name, the age, the deserts, the dignities, the state, *the praises both of body and mind*, the good and bad fortunes in the life and the manner and time of the death of the person therein interred". This account of an Epitaph . . . as far as it goes is just . . . (*Prose Works*, ii, pp. 88–9; the italics are Wordsworth's)

In Chiabrera's longer epitaphs the reader learns of the moral and intellectual excellence of those who are being commemorated "by a brief history of the course of their lives, or a selection of events and circumstances" and in this way the dead are "individualized", but with the modifying effects of "commiseration" and "praises". Johnson's "On the Death of Dr. Robert Levet" and Wordsworth's portraits in Books V, VI and VII of *The Excursion* are (in Wordsworth's phrase) "characteristic and circumstantial"; in them individual and general truth are reconciled and a fine balance or synthesis of opposites is achieved.

4 The Poem as Epitaph

> In them [epitaphs] love was shewed to
> the deceased, memorie was continued to
> posteritie, friends were comforted, and the
> Reader put in mind of human frailtie.
>
> John Weever (1631)

The "fine balance of truth in observing, with the imaginative faculty in modifying, the objects observed" is only one of the many reconciliations which Coleridge noticed in Wordsworth's poetry; the same sentence comments on the "union of deep feeling with profound thought" which had so impressed him in *Lyrical Ballads*.[1] In a later chapter of *Biographia Literaria* he records how his early conversations with Wordsworth "turned frequently on the two cardinal points of poetry" (which when successfully achieved became one). These were "faithful adherence to the truth of nature, and the power of giving the interest of novelty by the modifying colours of imagination." This is later rephrased more simply: "Mr. Wordsworth . . . was to propose to himself as his object, to give the charm of novelty to things of every day."[2] In Chapter 22 Coleridge lists what he considers to be Wordsworth's characteristic defects and excellences. These opposing lists are sometimes taken as the source of the "Two Voices" theory of Wordsworth's poetry:

> Two voices are there: one is of the deep . . .
> And one is of an old half-witted sheep
> Which bleats articulate monotony,
> And indicates that two and one are three . . .
> And, Wordsworth, both are thine . . .[3]

It is, of course, true that Coleridge does not ever see

Wordsworth's best work as somehow miraculously synthesising these faults and virtues into a new and greater excellence; he is certain that wherever the faults occur they spoil the poetry. He would not have accepted, I think, the upgrading of Wordswoth's "matter-of-factness" and "laborious minuteness" into what F. W. Bateson calls "an essentially objective poetry, evincing a strong sense of social responsibility, but crude, naive and often bathetic (the Augustan manner)"; nor would he have accepted that this voice was necessary or present in Wordsworth's finest work. It may be true that Wordsworth is "not at heart either an Augustan master or a Romantic master. The peculiarity of his poetry is that it oscillates between the two styles," or, more accurately, that "the poems are Augustan *and* Romantic"; but the Augustan manner has nothing to do with the poetry's occasional "thick-ankled" quality.[4] There were things which Wordsworth did not wish to reconcile. In 1831 he writes that

> it is next to impossible entirely to harmonise things that rest upon their poetic credibility, and are idealised by distance of time and space, with those that rest upon the evidence of the hour, and have about them the thorny points of actual life. (*LY*, ii, p. 580)

As Coleridge makes clear, Wordsworth's excellences are themselves a synthesis of different or opposing qualities. He "may be mimicked by copyists", but, says Coleridge, "he cannot be imitated, except by those who are not born to be imitators"; the synthesis which is his success is too difficult for imitation:

> For without his depth of feeling and his imaginative power his *sense* would want its vital warmth and peculiarity; and without his strong sense, his *mysticism* would become *sickly* – mere fog, and dimness![5]

Coleridge praises the "austere purity of language both grammatically and logically" (the Augustan manner) but it is "framed to convey not the object alone, but likewise the character, mood and intentions of the person who is representing it". Again, "the weight and sanity of the Thoughts and Sentiments" which are won "from the poet's own meditative observation" are at the same time "*fresh* and have the dew upon them". A fourth excellence which Coleridge finds in Wordsworth is "the perfect truth of nature in his images and descriptions as taken immediately from nature"; but this is only possible because of the poet's "genial intimacy with the very spirit which gives the physiognomic expression to all the works of nature". In a key Wordsworth image Coleridge suggests that his "perfect truth of nature" is a reconcilement of outer and inner, of fact modified by imagination: "Like a green field reflected in a calm and perfectly transparent lake, the image is distinguished from the reality only by its greater softness and lustre." The fifth excellence is, as Coleridge describes it, a bringing together of opposites; it is "a meditative pathos, a union of deep and subtle thought and sensibility". The final and greatest quality which Coleridge finds is "Imagination in the highest and strictest sense of the word". It is the function of imagination, he says in an earlier chapter, "to idealize and to unify. It is essentially *vital*, even as all objects (*as* objects) are essentially fixed and dead". It is the imagination ("that synthetic and magical power" which Wordsworth supremely possesses) which

> reveals itself in the balance or reconcilement of opposite or discordant qualities: of sameness, with difference; of the general with the concrete; the idea with the image; the individual with the representative; the sense of novelty and freshness with old and familiar objects; a more than usual state of emotion with more than usual order; judgment ever awake and steady self-possession with enthusiasm and feeling profound or vehement . . . it blends and harmonizes the natural and the artificial.[6]

I have tried to show in the previous chapters how Wordsworth, especially in the *Essays upon Epitaphs*, saw such reconcilement of opposites as the aim and purpose of his poetry, and that the greatest virtue of the epitaph was its ability to unify things separate and to bring together discordant qualities in all the ways that Coleridge suggests, and in ways that he does not mention. It is, indeed, the very nature of the epitaph that it should so comprehensively and triumphantly reconcile.

As we saw in the first chapter, the epitaph brings together the several publics which a poet might have or wish to have. It is not "a proud writing shut up for the studious; it is exposed to all"; a stranger who reads it is introduced "through its mediation to the company of a friend". It records a private grief, but with its traditional words "Halt, Traveller!", speaks publicly to all men; "it is concerning all and for all". An epitaph reconciles *pathos* and *ethos*, or (to use Wordsworth's terms) it combines energy with stillness, grandeur with tenderness. It reconciles "a more than usual state of emotion with more than usual order"; in an epitaph "the passions should be subdued, the emotions controlled; strong indeed but nothing ungovernable or wholly involuntary. Seemliness requires this and truth requires it also: for how can the narrator otherwise be trusted?" An epitaph reconciles the general with the particular; "The general sympathy ought to be quickened . . . by particular thoughts, images", and these "two powers" ought to "temper, restrain and exalt each other." A parish church with its churchyard is "a visible centre of community of the living and the dead" and this community can be vividly established in an epitaph where the dead man is considered to be speaking directly to those who stop to read. "By this tender fiction, the survivors bind themselves to a sedater sorrow", and the fiction is possible through "the intervention of the imagination in order that the reason may speak her own language earlier than she would otherwise have been enabled to do". It is imagination (whose merit, said Coleridge, is to blend and fuse and unify) which does this; it is the "shadowy interposition" of imagination which, in an epitaph, "harmoniously unites the two worlds of the living and the dead" and reconciles reason and passion into a "sedater sorrow".[7] "Genuine knowledge", says Wordsworth in *The Prelude*, grows from "those sweet counsels between head and heart."[8] In a note to one of his

Itinerary Poems of 1833 Wordsworth declares his approval of
prayers for the dead, "the barriers between the two worlds
dissolving before the power of love and faith".⁹ "Dissolving" the
barriers between two worlds is at the heart of Wordsworth's
thinking and poetry and, in particular, dissolving the distinction
(in order later to reunite them) between what we would normally
consider the living and the lifeless, the animate and inanimate.
This is behind, for example, the comments on the figure of the old
man and the images of the "huge stone" and the cloud in
"Resolution and Independence"¹⁰ and it is at the heart of the
passage in *The Prelude* (very clearly an epitaph when it was first
published as a separate poem in 1800) where the boy blows owl-
calls. As he waits expectantly for the birds to answer,

. . . a gentle shock of mild surprise
Has carried far into his heart the voice
Of mountain torrents; or the visible scene
Would enter unawares into his mind,
With all its solemn imagery, its rocks,
Its woods, and that uncertain heaven, received
Into the bosom of the steady lake. (*The Prelude*, 1850, v, ll. 382–8)

Outer and inner melt into a single new awareness or perception;
the active or living "would enter" is not to be distinguished from
the passive or lifeless "received".

In the Preface to *Lyrical Ballads* Wordsworth had said that he
could not give the reader a more exact notion of the style in which
it was his intention to write, "than by informing him that I have
at all times endeavoured to look steadily at my subject". In many
poems he brings to the reader's notice these recurring moments of
attention: "I gazed and gazed" (repeated in several poems);
"Upon the moon I fixed my eye"; "I listened motionless and
still"; "I fixed my view"; "while he hung listening". The
moment of attention *is* that act of the imagination which by its
"modifying colours" "dissolves, diffuses, dissipates" the poet's
initially "faithful adherence to the truth of nature" in order to
"re-create" or "to idealize and to unify" that truth. This

unifying, reconciling power is, in an epitaph, taken over by love; for an act of intense attention (love) towards someone dead is the inspiration of every epitaph. The writer of an epitaph composes "by the side of the grave . . . of one whom he loves and admires". Wordsworth accepts John Weever's inclusive, reconciling description of an epitaph, that in it "love was shewed to the deceased, memorie was continued to posteritie, friends were comforted, and the Reader put in mind of humane frailtie". It is in the epitaph that through the transforming, modifying power of imagination, or love, we can see Wordsworth most clearly and typically "poised between a realist reading of the world and a purely subjective one".[11]

Phrase after phrase describes and confirms the role of this "modifying power". "The light of love in our hearts is a satisfactory evidence that there is a body of worth in the minds of our friends or kindred, whence that light has proceeded."[12] As we saw in an earlier chapter, the character of a dead person ("the truth of nature") must be seen through a "tender haze" – that is, lovingly – or "luminous mist". This luminosity is the brightness of a profounder truth; "It *is* truth, and of the highest order . . . it is truth hallowed by love". An epitaph reconciles subjective and objective; it is the "joint offspring of the worth of the dead and the affections of the living". In an epitaph the "quality of the mind of a virtuous man" will appear in it, and be felt "as something midway between what he was on earth walking about with his living frailties, and what he may be presumed to be as a Spirit in heaven".[13] (Much of Wordsworth's poetry, whether "Daffodils", "Tintern Abbey" or *The Prelude*, combines an interest in the object itself, "truth to nature", with the modifying process or perception by the mind in an act of attention.) Human beings cannot be "profitably looked at or described" without love; and the "encomiastic language" of epitaphs in a country churchyard is not so far from the truth as might be supposed, since the writers of them saw the dead through the luminosity of love, through "that medium of love, sorrow, and admiration" which "softens down or removes" the "harshness and contradictions" which made up the mixture of good and evil in their lives on earth.[14]

A failure in an epitaph is a failure of imagination or love, for the two can scarcely be separated. Wordsworth comments on an epitaph which records the death of a sick woman who had gone to Bristol in the vain hope that she might recover by drinking its mineral springs. Wordsworth says of one line that it "flows nobly from the heart and the imagination". Of another line, "She bowed to taste the wave and died", he says that the expression involves "petty occupations for the fancy"; the reader is given a shock of surprise, "entertaining perhaps to a light fancy, but to a steady mind unsatisfactory – because false".[15] In an epitaph on Sir George Vane, Wordsworth finds fault with the line "He was Sir George once but St. George ever", because it seems likely that in it "the Author prided himself upon what he might call a clever hit"; his "better affections" were not involved, but "his vanity delighted with the act of ingenuity by which they had been combined".[16] The word "combined" suggests the functioning of the Fancy. For Coleridge the Fancy could assemble and juxtapose images ("the act of ingenuity by which they had been combined") but could not fuse or reconcile them; the images of Fancy have "no connexion, natural or moral, but are yoked together by the poet by means of some occasional coincidence".[17] The "steady mind" ("I have at all times endeavoured to look steadily at my subject") can rest only on the stability of truth which is found in an act of undivided attention. The "vanity" of the epitaph on Sir George Vane is a deflection of that attention and is a failure, however momentary, of imagination and love. A good epitaph, it seems, cannot be the product of Fancy, but only of Imagination.

"Love" and "imagination" are interchangeable terms in the *Essays*; certainly love now has the function of imagination. Love in an epitaph works with and through the power of memory, for a memory is created by love or attention. A churchyard with its many epitaphs is "decorated . . . by the hand of Memory, and shining, if I may so say, in the light of love".[18] An epitaph is an act of memory (a recollection in tranquillity) and through memory even personal hostility disappears: "Enmity melts away; as it disappears, unsightliness, disproportion and deformity vanish; and through the influence of commiseration, a harmony of love and beauty succeeds." Through this power of love are

Deposited upon the silent shore
Of memory, images and present thoughts,
That shall not die and cannot be destroyed. (*The Excursion*, vii, ll. 28–30)

John Weever found that in an epitaph "memorie was continued to posteritie"; the past is modified by memory in the present writing of an epitaph for future consolation:

I would enshrine the spirit of the past
For future restoration. (*The Prelude*, 1805, xi, ll. 342–3)

The epitaph records an event in time but also, through memory, out of time; it reconciles past, present and future. "To remember was, for Wordsworth, to be a poet";[19] the epitaph emerges as a Wordsworthian "spot of time". It is imagination or love which creates memory; Wordsworth objected to a poet who went out walking with a notebook and pencil to record what he saw, "went home, and wove the whole together into a poetical description":

But Nature does not permit an inventory to be made of her charms! He should have left his pencil and notebook at home; fixed his eyes, as he walked, with a reverent attention on all that surrounded him, and taken all into a heart that could understand and enjoy. Then, after several days had passed by, he should have interrogated his memory as to the scene. He would have discovered that while much of what he had admired was preserved to him, much was also wisely obliterated. That which remained – the picture surviving in his mind – would have presented the ideal and essential truth of the scene, and done so, in a large part, by discarding much which, though in itself striking, was not characteristic.[20]

The poet's failure was a failure of attention (he should have
"fixed his eye") and a failure of love; he did not look at things
with "reverent attention" and so could not take them into his
heart. The poet "wove" all he saw together "into a poetic
description" (the mechanical operation of Fancy) instead of
letting "reverent attention" work through memory ("after
several days have passed") to create something new, "the ideal
and essential truth of the scene" (an act of Imagination):

> So feeling comes in aid
> Of feeling, and diversity of strength
> Attends us, if but once we have been strong. (*The Prelude*, 1850,
>   xii, ll. 269–71)

The epitaph emerges as the quintessential poem, or as the
epitome of what Wordsworth considers the truest poetry. We do
not need to read this into the *Essays upon Epitaphs*: Wordsworth
there makes very clear that in talking of epitaphs and the writers
of epitaphs he is talking of poets and poetry, and usually of
himself and his own poetic practice. Any reader of epitaphs will
discover "that the faults predominant in the literature of every
age will be as strongly reflected in the sepulchral inscriptions as
any where".[21] Wordsworth's critical terms apply equally to
epitaphs and poetry; a certain epitaph is praised because the

> composition is a perfect whole; there is nothing arbitrary or
> mechanical, but it is an organized body of which the members
> are bound together by a common life and are all justly
> proportioned. (*Prose Works*, ii, p. 89)

It is a work of the Imagination ("nothing mechanical") and of
Art ("justly proportioned"), yet the imagery used, a body and its
members bound together by a common life, has a wonderful
appropriateness to the epitaph which reconciles past, present and
future and brings together into communion the dead, the living
and those as yet unborn. The purpose of an epitaph is to bring the
reader closer to "those primary sensations of the human heart,

which are the vital springs of sublime and pathetic composition, in this and in every other kind".[22] (The "Preface" to *Lyrical Ballads* claims that one intention of the poems was to trace "the primary laws of our nature".) Wordsworth's comments on epitaphs lead him to establish "a criterion of sincerity, by which a writer may be judged", since an epitaph "calls for sincerity more urgently than any other".[23] Sincerity in an epitaph, as in a poem, is born of imagination and love; insincerity in an epitaph is very quickly detected, for "the writer who would excite sympathy is bound in this case, more than in any other, to give proof that he himself has been moved".[24] (The poet, said Wordsworth in the 'Preface', looks at the world "in the spirit of love" and carries everywhere with him "relationship and love".) No faults have such "killing power" as those which prove that the writer of an epitaph is not in earnest and has "leisure for affectation", that he has not "fixed his eye" on his subject. A bad epitaph, like a bad poem, results from failures in sensibility and "errors in taste and judgement".[25] Through an examination of epitaphs Wordsworth believes he can best persuade the reader that "the excellence of writing, whether in prose or verse, consists in a conjunction of Reason and Passion"; certainly "the tyranny of bad taste" can be brought home most powerfully by showing that our natural feelings can yield to it when we are showing to our dead friends what ought in an epitaph to be a "solemn testimony of love".[26] "Upon a call so urgent", says Wordsworth of the epitaph, but in words which describe his own characteristic practice, "it might be expected that the affections, the memory, and the imagination would be constrained to speak their genuine language."[27] An epitaph is, supremely, emotion recollected in tranquillity; Wordsworth's declaration in the Preface that the poet has "a disposition to be affected more than other men by absent things as if they were present"[28] will be particularly true when the poet is composing an epitaph. It is not enough for the writer to show that he has been moved himself; he must remember that "to raise a monument is a sober and reflective act" and that an epitaph is "intended to be permanent, and for universal perusal". Therefore if the thoughts and feelings expressed are also to be permanent, they must be "liberated from that weakness and anguish of sorrow which is in its nature transitory, and which with instinctive decency retires from notice". Moral and artistic decorum are here reconciled, and from this reconciliation achieved through the operation of memory is born Wordsworth's poetry of understatement or "moving restraint". Epitaphs, like poems, are

> Woven out of passion's sharpest agonies,
> Subdued, composed, and formalized by art,
> To fix a wiser sorrow in the heart. (*PW*, iv, p. 27)

The "art" (both meanings of the word are apt[29]) is in the "composing". The feelings must be subdued and "the emotions controlled; strong, indeed, but nothing ungovernable or wholly involuntary. Seemliness requires this, and truth requires it also."[30] In the *Essay, Supplementary to the Preface* Wordsworth's description of the "higher poetry" confirms his comments on the nature and value of the epitaph; in such poetry the reader will find "a reflection of the wisdom of the heart and the grandeur of the imagination. Wherever these appear, simplicity accompanies them".[31]

An epitaph tells of loss and separation and records the greatest of all commonplaces, death; it reminds the reader that death comes to every man, but speaks of one particular death and of the grief (and hope) of those who still live. It is as true of epitaphs as of the poems in Lyrical Ballads that (as Wordsworth said in the Preface) "the feeling therein developed gives importance to the action and situation, and not the action and situation to the feeling". The death of someone loved is one of those "situations from common life" which were to be the subject of *Lyrical Ballads*; and as "a certain colouring of imagination" was to be thrown over the situations in those poems in order that they might be "carried alive into the heart of passion", so the same imagination will give to death and loss and grief "a pathos and a spirit which shall re-admit them into the soul like revelations of the moment". The epitaph, like so many of Wordsworth's poems, is the "symbolic reverberation of a commonplace and accidental situation";[32] very often in his poetry, and always in an epitaph, the accidental situation is death. An epitaph is the public expression of a private loss; it is a generalised expression of every man's own experience of "the mighty gulf of separation"; and by recording that gulf it seeks to bridge it. An epitaph continues memory to posterity; it speaks of death and of a continued life in memory and hope; as in "Tintern Abbey" Wordsworth laments the death of the "aching joys" and "dizzy raptures" of the days when nature was "all in all" to him, but dares to hope

> That in this moment there is life and food
> For future years.

Hazlitt described Wordsworth's poems as "mournful *requiems* over the grave of human hopes". From the steady contemplation of loss, separation, death, comes much of his finest work, but expressed in such a wide variety of ways that we scarcely notice how persistently he is concerned with

> The memory of what has been,
> And never more will be.

In *The Borderers* (composed 1796–7) Marmaduke unwittingly perpetrates a great crime. In the Preface to the play Wordsworth refers to what Rousseau had said about the destructive instincts of the child and goes on to describe Oswald as one "who lays waste the groves that should shelter him". A year later, in "Nutting", Wordsworth puts all this together and tells of the day in childhood when he literally laid waste the groves. For Marmaduke and Wordsworth this great crime against nature resulted in loss, the loss of innocence or, more exactly, of unself-consciousness; but the loss in Wordsworth's poetry can be of many different things. Poems as different as "The Last of the Flock", "Michael", "Alice Fell", "The Two April Mornings", the last of "The River Duddon" sonnets, "Tintern Abbey", "Poor Susan", "The Ruined Cottage" and the "Elegiac

Stanzas" on Peele Castle all speak of loss or dereliction or separation or death. It may be a shepherd's loss of his flock, or of his son; or it may be a man's loss of his brother and separation after many years from the community which nurtured them, or a small girl's loss of her cloak of duffil grey, or of "a splendour in the objects of sense which is passed away". As we read Wordsworth we come to understand that seldom,

> Even for the least division of an hour,
> Have I been so beguiled as to be blind
> To my most grievous loss. (*PW*, iii, p. 161)

It is not only in the poems that loss and separation move him to memorable speech. In the *Reply to "Mathetes"* (1809–10) the wonderful image of the extinguished candle is "an intimation and an image of departing human life",[34] and two unforgettable phrases from the *Letters* are on the death of his brother, "The set is now broken", and on Dorothy's mental collapse, "My dear ruin of a Sister". In a note in 1843 to a sonnet written in 1815, Wordsworth says that "I could write a treatise of lamentation upon the changes brought about among the cottages of Westmoreland by the silence of the Spinning-wheel".[35]

Critics have used biographical details of many kinds to explain such an elegiac emphasis; we are reminded that he lost his mother when he was only eight and that his last sight of her was as she lay on her death-bed; that many years later he became separated from Annette Vallon, and that in 1805 his favourite brother John was drowned. Then there are more intangible biographical explanations. Wordsworth tells us that he lost "that dream-like vividness and splendour which invest objects of sight in childhood"; Coleridge said of "A slumber did my spirit seal", that "Some months ago Wordsworth transmitted to me a most sublime epitaph. Whether it had any reality I cannot say. Most probably, in some gloomier moment he had fancied the moment in which his sister might die."[36] The Oxford editor picks up Coleridge's tentative comment, treats it as if it were fact and offers it as a probable explanation of another "Lucy" poems, "She

dwelt among the untrodden ways": "this poem had probably a
similar source. And the fact that it was written at Goslar, when he
was in her company, supports the conclusion."[37] It might seem,
however, just as likely for Wordsworth to have this fear when he
was *not* with his sister; it is when the lover is separated from his
sweetheart in "Strange fits of passion have I known" that he fears
and imagines she may be dead. More valuable and interesting
is Wordsworth's remark in a note to "Intimations of Immortality":

> I was often unable to think of external things as having
> external existence, and I communed with all that I saw as
> something not apart from, but inherent in, my own immaterial
> nature. Many times while going to school have I grasped at a
> wall or tree to recall myself from this abyss of idealism to the
> reality. (*PW*, iv, p. 463)

Solipsism is the most terrifying separation or loss of all. But
biographical explanation leads nowhere. (The genesis of "The
Solitary Reaper" should be sufficient warning against making
too facile a connection between poem and fact. Wordsworth did
not meet the girl, but read about her in Thomas Wilkinson's *Tour
of Scotland*.)[38] The "Elegiac Stanzas" on Peele Castle were
composed shortly after the death of his brother ("Him whom I
deplore") and directly because of it; but even here what is most
passionately and memorably lamented is something less immediate and tangible:

> A power is gone which nothing can restore.

In these stanzas the drowned brother John has indeed suffered a
sea-change, into something rich and strange. If loss and death
and separation and "fallings from us . . . vanishings" moved
Wordsworth to marvellous utterance, the explanation is not in
the facts of such death or separation. He had the imagination of
loss anterior to nearly any experience of loss. Among his Juvenilia
are a "Dirge" and poems on a drowned dog and the death of a

starling. An epitaph was a means of giving to a generalised or unfocused imaginative feeling of loss a local habitation and a name.

But an epitaph does not speak only of death; "The invention of epitaphs, Weever, in his Discourse of Funeral Monuments, says rightly, 'proceeded from the presage or fore-feeling of immortality, implanted in all men naturally'." An epitaph is at first the record of loss, but this goes with "a humble expression of Christian confidence in immortality". An epitaph is "a record to preserve the memory of the dead"; it is when a man is "under the pressure of sorrow" for the deaths of those he loves that he seeks to prolong their memory in an epitaph, and wishes "to preserve for future times vestiges of the departed".[39] An epitaph expresses the hope of resurrection or immortality and also the secular immortality conferred by memory alone. What was dead is alive again through memory. Through the working of memory sorrow is turned into joy; as even

> In terror,
> Remembered terror, there is peace and rest. (*PW*, i, p. 186)

An epitaph is for Wordsworth the epitome of poetry because it is analogous to the "spot of time" and his own poetic mode. (The "spot of time" is not confined to *The Prelude*; the phrase defines many of his poems.) If the experience that he records in his poetry is very often the sense of loss, we might say that in the epitaph and in the poem as epitaph the "function of memory was to impose on experience the control of art: to distance both poet and reader from reality in such a way as to transfigure painful or shocking events and heighten their meaning".[40] Memory can be defined as Wordsworth defined imagination, "the faculty which produces impressive effects out of simple elements".[41] The transfiguration, like the "spot of time", is the reconcilement of opposites. Through memory an epitaph reconciles time and eternity; it records an event in time and by recording it removes it from time, and makes of the past a perpetual present:

Matthew is in his grave, yet now,
Methinks, I see him stand,
As at that moment . . . (*PW*, iv, p. 71)

Wordsworth's description and definition of the "spot of time",
of time' is in the eleventh book of the 1805 version of *The Prelude*:

There are in our existence spots of time,
Which with distinct pre-eminence retain
A vivifying virtue . . . (*The Prelude*, 1805, xi, ll. 258–60)

The last phrase, weakened in the 1850 version to "renovating
virtue", suggests the mighty force of these "spots of time", these
moments of acute attention when the poet, in Shelley's phrase
"imagines what he knows" and which, when recollected, are a
source of joy and power, by which

              our minds
Are nourished and invisibly repaired.

"Vivifying" has the force of "giving new life to"; it is that
immortality hoped for in an epitaph and already achieved there
in the love and memory of the living. "Virtue" (I quote from the
OED) is "the power or operative influence inherent in a
supernatural or divine being"; it is the transfiguring which can
more properly be called Imagination. Wordsworth goes on to
give an example of a "spot of time". He describes a separation; as
a small boy he had been out riding with "honest James", but
"some mischance Disjoined me from my comrade". The boy
finds himself near the ruins of a gibbet at the spot where

Some unknown hand had carved the murderer's name.
The monumental writing was engraven
In times long past; and still, from year to year,
By superstition of the neighbourhood,
The grass is cleared away, and to this hour
The letters are all fresh and visible. (ll. 294–9)

This epitaph within the spot of time has kept alive the past into the present for, as we shall see, the transfiguration of the future. The terrified boy leaves the spot:

> And, reascending the bare common, saw
> A naked pool that lay beneath the hills,
> The beacon on the summit, and more near,
> A girl who bore a pitcher on her head,
> And seemed with difficult steps to force her way
> Against the blowing wind. It was, in truth
> An ordinary sight; but I should need
> Colours and words that are unknown to man,
> To paint the visionary dreariness
> Which, while I looked all round for my lost guide
> Did at that time invest the naked pool,
> The beacon on the lonely eminence,
> The woman and her garments vexed and tossed
> By the strong wind. (ll. 303–16)

The visionary moment emerges, as always, from a moment of attention: "I looked all round for my lost guide". Many years later, "in the blessed time of early love", the poet revisits the place "With those two dear ones, to my heart so dear", and upon the same scene now falls

> The spirit of pleasure and youth's golden gleam;
> And think ye not with radiance more divine
> From these remembrances, and from the power
> They left behind? (ll. 323–6)

From "remembrance" comes new "power":

> so feeling comes in aid
> Of feeling, and diversity of strength
> Attends us, if but once we have been strong. (ll. 326–8)

To have been strong is to have imagined, or paid attention, or loved; the feeling that "comes in aid" of this first feeling is the transfiguration and reconcilement gained through the secular grace of memory.

Wordsworth's later poetry is seldom the poetry of epitaphs. He ceased, in his poetry, to look steadily at his subject and therefore could no longer carry his pitcher to the well of memory. His poetry was no longer a reconcilement of opposites but a denial of opposites. It became less personal and more egotistic. The later verse has neither the "lapidary precision" nor the "imaginative tension" which he had considered to be the essential qualities of epitaphs and poetry (and which he had failed to find in the work of Crabbe). A change like this cannot be dated; it came from a loss which this time he did not express, but which he prophesied in *The Prelude*:

> The days gone by
> Come back upon me from the dawn almost
> Of life: the hiding-places of my power
> Seem open; I approach, and then they close;
> I see by glimpses now; when age comes on,
> May scarcely see at all . . . (*The Prelude*, 1805, xi, ll. 334–9)

The White Doe of Rylstone (written 1807–8, published 1815), though symbolist and external, is perhaps Wordsworth's last great poem in the mode of epitaph. The story is one of shocking loss; Richard Norton and his nine sons are killed in the rebellion of the Northern earls in 1569. In a note to the poem in 1843 Wordsworth says that Emily, the heroine of the poem and sole survivor of the family, learns

> To abide
> The shock, and finally secure
> O'er pain and grief a triumph pure.

He explains that

> She achieves this not without aid from the communication

with the inferior Creature, which often leads her thoughts to revolve upon the past with a tender and humanizing influence that exalts rather than depresses her. (*PW*, iii, p. 543)

This, as we saw, is also the virtue of the epitaph or "spot of time". The "inferior Creature" who provides this aid is the White Doe, and the White Doe is a symbol of memory. Emily alone survives of the family, but survives at first in something like despair:

> And she *hath* wandered, long and far
> Beneath the light of sun and star;
> Hath roamed in trouble and in grief,
> Driven forward like a withered leaf,
> Yea, like a ship at random blown
> To distant places and unknown. (ll. 1611–16)

Despair gives way to stoicism:

> Her soul doth in itself stand fast . . .
> Undaunted, lofty, calm and stable. (ll. 1623, 1627)

At this point the Doe appears,

> And laid its head upon her knee
> And looked into the Lady's face,
> A look of pure benignity,
> And fond unclouded memory. (ll. 1654–7)

This deep memory humanises Emily's soul:

> And, by her gushing thoughts subdued,
> She melted into tears –
> A flood of tears that flowed apace
> Upon the happy Creature's face. (ll. 1661–4)

The White Doe is

This lovely chronicler of things
Long past, delights and sorrowings.
Lone Sufferer! will not she [Emily] believe
The promise in that speaking face;
And welcome, as a gift of grace,
The saddest thought the Creature brings? (ll. 1674–9)

This gift of grace is memory. As Emily goes everywhere with the Doe she is "cheered and fortified"; ("so feeling comes in aid of feeling"), and with the grace of memory the past is no longer terrible; ("In terror/Remembered terror, there is peace and rest"); Emily can at last come home to Rylstone, can come home, with the Doe, to that past from which she had tried to flee:

With her Companion, in such frame
Of mind, to Rylstone back she came;
And, ranging through the wasted groves,
Received the memory of old loves,
Undisturbed and undistrest. (ll. 1751–5)

Even the death of her favourite brother Francis can now have a "vivifying virtue" as she visits his grave in Bolton Abbey, always "Attended by the soft-paced Doe":

For that she came; there oft she sate
Forlorn, but not disconsolate;
And, when she from the abyss returned
Of thought, she neither shrunk nor mourned;
Was happy that she lived to greet
Her mute Companion as it lay
In love and pity at her feet. (ll. 1819–25)

All this, however, is from the final canto, and like many of Wordsworth's poems this one begins at the end. In the first canto, long before we learn of the history of the Nortons (and long after the rebellion and its tragedy are over), the mysterious Doe makes her appearance. Like imagination, she

Sheds on the flowers that round her blow
A more than sunny liveliness. (ll. 104–5)

The Doe (like the epitaph) speaks to all, to that comprehensive
audience which Wordsworth had so long wanted, to

> . . . a variegated band
> Of middle-aged, and old, and young,
> And little children by the hand
> Upon their leading mothers hung. (ll. 162–5)

What she speaks to them, or rather, what she reminds them of, is
the past:

> . . . all the standers-by,
> Could tell a tragic history
> Of facts divulged, wherein appear
> Substantial motive, reason clear,
> Why thus the milk-white Doe is found
> Couchant beside that lonely mound. (ll. 198–203)

She offers to the living what years before she offered to the now
long dead Emily,

> A softened remembrance of sorrow and pain. (l. 240)

and also

> . . . recollections clear and bright;
> Which yet do unto some impart
> An undisturbed repose of heart. (ll. 317–19)

Wordsworth said that the poem was about "the Apotheosis of the
Animal":

> It starts from a high point of imagination, and comes round
> through various wanderings of that faculty to a still higher;

nothing less than the Apotheosis of the Animal . . . And as the poem thus begins and ends, with pure and lofty Imagination, every motive and impulse that actuates the persons introduced is from the same source, a kindred spirit pervades, and is intended to harmonize the whole. (*MY*, ii, p. 276)

The poem begins and ends, we recall, with the Doe, and the Doe is imagination; like the epitaph and the spot of time the Doe "bears a memory" and reconciles many opposites. Wordsworth said that the Doe was imagination; if I have said that the Doe is also memory, it is simply to insist that for Wordsworth memory *is* imagination, and that when he imagines the Abbey saying to the Doe, long after Emily's death, .and in the closing lines of the poem,

> Thou, thou art not a child of time,

it speaks of memory and of imagination and of the poem as epitaph.

Appendix:
Dr Johnson, *An Essay on Epitaphs* (1740)

Though criticism has been cultivated in every age of learning, by men of great abilities and extensive knowledge, till the rules of writing are become rather burdensome than instructive to the mind; though almost every species of composition has been the subject of particular treatises, and given birth to definitions, distinctions, precepts and illustrations; yet no critick of note, that has fallen within my observation, has hitherto thought sepulchral inscriptions worthy of a minute examination, or pointed out, with proper accuracy, their beauties and defects.

The reasons of this neglect it is useless to inquire, and, perhaps, impossible to discover; it might be justly expected that this kind of writing would have been the favourite topick of criticism, and that self-love might have produced some regard for it, in those authors that have crowded libraries with elaborate disssertations upon Homer; since to afford a subject for heroick poems is the privilege of very few, but every man may expect to be recorded in an epitaph, and, therefore, finds some interest in providing that his memory may not suffer by an unskilful panegyrick.

If our prejudices in favour of antiquity deserve to have any part in the regulation of our studies, epitaphs seem entitled to more than common regard, as they are, probably, of the same age with the art of writing. The most ancient structures in the world, the pyramids, are supposed to be sepulchral monuments, with either pride or gratitude erected; and the same passions which incited men to such laborious and expensive methods of preserving their own memory, or that of their benefactors, would, doubtless, incline them not to neglect any easier means by which the same ends might be obtained. Nature and reason have dictated to every nation, that to preserve good actions from oblivion, is both the interest and duty of mankind: and, therefore, we find no people acquainted with the use of letters, that omitted to grace the tombs of their heroes and wise men with panegyrical inscriptions.

To examine, therefore, in what the perfection of epitaphs consists, and what rules are to be observed in composing them, will be, at least, of as much use as other critical inquiries; and for assigning a few hours to such disquisitions, great examples, at least, if not strong reasons, may be pleaded.

An epitaph, as the word itself implies, is an inscription on a tomb, and, in its most extensive import, may admit, indiscriminately, satire or praise. But as malice has seldom produced monuments of defamation, and the tombs, hitherto raised, have been the work of friendship and benevolence, custom has contracted the original latitude of the word, so that it signifies, in the general acceptation, an inscription engraven on a tomb in honour of the person deceased.

As honours are paid to the dead, in order to incite others to the imitation of their excellencies, the principal intention of epitaphs is to perpetuate the examples of virtue, that the tomb of a good man may supply the want of his presence, and veneration for his memory produce the same effect as the observation of his life. Those epitaphs are, therefore, the most perfect, which set virtue in the strongest light, and are best adapted to exalt the reader's ideas, and rouse his emulation.

To this end it is not always necessary to recount the actions of a hero, or enumerate the writings of a philosopher; to imagine such informations necessary, is to detract from their characters, or to suppose their works mortal, or their achievements in danger of being forgotten. The bare name of such men answers every purpose of a long inscription.

Had only the name of Sir Isaac Newton been subjoined to the design upon his monument, instead of a long detail of his discoveries, which no philosopher can want, and which none but a philosopher can understand, those, by whose direction it was raised, had done more honour both to him and to themselves.

This, indeed, is a commendation which it requires no genius to bestow, but which can never become vulgar or contemptible, if bestowed with judgement; because no single age produces many men of merit superiour to panegyrick. None but the first names can stand unassisted against the attacks of time; and if men raised to reputation by accident or caprice, have nothing but their names engraved on their tombs, there is danger lest, in a few years, the inscription require an interpreter. Thus have their expectations been disappointed who honoured Picus of Mirandola with this pompous epitaph:

> His situs est PICUS MIRANDOLA, caetera norunt
> Et Tagus et Ganges, forsan et Antipodes.

His name, then celebrated in the remotest corners of the earth, is now almost forgotten; and his works, then studied, admired, and applauded, are now mouldering in obscurity.

Next in dignity to the bare name is a short character simple and unadorned, without exaggeration, superlatives, or rhetorick. Such were the inscriptions in use among the Romans, in which the victories gained by their emperours were commemorated by a single epithet; as Cæsar Germanicus, Cæsar Dacicus, Germanicus, Illyricus. Such would be this epitaph, ISAACUS NEWTONUS, naturæ legibus investigatis, hic quiescit.

But to far the greatest part of mankind a longer encomium is necessary for the publication of their virtues, and the preservation of their memories; and, in the composition of these it is, that art is principally required, and precepts, therefore, may be useful.

In writing epitaphs, one circumstance is to be considered, which affects no other composition; the place in which they are now commonly found restrains them to a particular air of solemnity, and debars them from the admission of all lighter or gayer ornaments. In this, it is that, the style of an epitaph necessarily differs from that of an elegy. The customs of burying our dead, either in or near our churches, perhaps, originally founded on a rational design of fitting the mind for religious exercises, by laying before it the most affecting proofs of the uncertainty of life, makes it proper to exclude from our epitaphs all such allusions as are contrary to the doctrines, for the propagation of which the churches are erected, and to the end for which those who peruse the monuments must be supposed to come thither. Nothing is, therefore, more ridiculous than to copy the Roman inscriptions, which were engraven on stones by the highway, and composed by those who generally reflected on mortality only to excite in themselves and others a quicker relish of pleasure, and a more luxurious enjoyment of life, and whose regard for the dead extended no farther than a wish that "the earth might be light upon them".

All allusions to the heathen mythology are, therefore, absurd, and all regard for the senseless remains of a dead man impertinent and superstitious. One of the first distinctions of the primitive Christians, was their neglect of bestowing garlands on the dead, in which they are very rationally defended by their apologist in Manutius Felix. "We lavish no flowers nor odours on the dead," says he, "because they have no sense of fragrance or of beauty." We profess to reverence the dead, not for their sake, but for our own. It is, therefore, always with indignation or contempt that I read the epitaph on Cowley, a man whose learning and poetry were his lowest merits:

> Aurea dum late volitant tua scripta per orbem,
> Et fama eternum vivis, divine poeta,
> Hic placida jaceas requie, custodiat urnam,
> Cana fides, vigilentque perenni lampade musæ!
>
> Sit sacer ille locus, nec quis temerarius ausit
> Sacrilega turbare manu venerabile bustum.
> Intacti maneant, maneant per sæcula ducles
> COWLEII cineres, serventque immobile saxum.

To pray that the ashes of a friend may lie undisturbed, and that the divinities that favoured him in his life may watch for ever round him, to preserve his tomb from violation, and drive sacrilege away, is only rational in him who believes the soul interested in the repose of the body, and the powers which he invokes for its protection able to preserve it. To censure such expressions, as contrary to religion, or as remains of heathen superstition, would be too great a degree of severity. I condemn them only as uninstructive and unaffecting, as too ludicrous for reverence or grief, for Christianity and a temple.

That the designs and decorations of monuments ought, likewise, to be formed with the same regard to the solemnity of the place, cannot be denied; it is an established principle, that all ornaments owe their beauty to their propriety. The same glitter of dress, that adds graces to gaiety and youth, would make age and dignity contemptible. Charon with his boat is far from heightening the awful grandeur of the universal judgement, though drawn by Angelo himself; nor is it easy to imagine a greater absurdity than that of gracing the walls of a Christian temple, with the figure of Mars leading a hero to battle, or Cupids sporting round a virgin. The pope who defaced the statues of the deities at the tomb of Sannazarius is, in my opinion, more easily to be defended, than he that erected them.

It is, for the same reason, improper to address the epitaph to the passenger, a custom which an injudicious veneration for antiquity introduced again at the revival of letters, and which, among many others, Passeratius suffered to mislead him in his epitaph upon the heart of Henry, king of France, who was stabbed by Clement the monk, which yet deserves to be inserted, for the sake of showing how beautiful even improprieties may become in the hands of a good writer:

> Adsta, viator, et dole regum vices.
> Cor regis isto conditur sub marmore,
> Qui jura Gallis, jura Sarmatis dedit;
> Tectus cucullo hunc sustulit sicarius.
> Abi, viator, et dole regum vices.

In the monkish ages, however ignorant and unpolished, the epitaphs were drawn up with far greater propriety than can be shown in those which more enlightened times have produced.

Orate pro anima miserrimi peccatoris,

was an address, to the last degree, striking and solemn, as it flowed naturally from the religion then believed, and awakened in the reader sentiments of benevolence for the deceased, and of concern for his own happiness. There was nothing trifling or ludicrous, nothing that did not tend to the noblest end, the propagation of piety, and the increase of devotion.

It may seem very superfluous to lay it down as the first rule for writing epitaphs, that the name of the deceased is not to be omitted; nor should I have thought such a precept necessary, had not the practice of the greatest writers shown, that it has not been sufficiently regarded. In most of the poetical epitaphs, the names for whom they were composed, may be sought to no purpose, being only prefixed on the monument. To expose the absurdity of this omission, it is only necessary to ask how the epitaphs, which have outlived the stones on which they were inscribed, would have contributed to the information of posterity, had they wanted the names of those whom they celebrated.

In drawing the character of the deceased, there are no rules to be observed which do not equally relate to other compositions. The praise ought not to be general, because the mind is lost in the extent of any indefinite idea, and cannot be affected with what it cannot comprehend. When we hear only of a good or great man, we know not in what class to place him, nor have any notion of his character, distinct from that of a thousand others; his example can have no effect upon our conduct, as we have nothing remarkable or eminent to propose to our imitation. The epitaph composed by Ennuis for his own tomb, has both the faults last mentioned.

Nemo me decoret lacrumis, nec funera fletu
Faxit. Cur? – Volito vivu' per ora virum.

The reader of this epitaph receives scarce any idea from it; he neither conceives any veneration for the man to whom it belongs, nor is instructed by what methods this boasted reputation is to be obtained.

Though a sepulchral inscription is professedly a panegyrick, and, therefore, not confined to historical impartiality, yet it ought always to be written with regard to truth. No man ought to be commended for virtues which he never possessed, but whoever is curious to know his faults must inquire after them in other places; the monuments of the dead are not intended to perpetuate the memory of crimes, but to exhibit patterns of virtue. On the tomb of Maecenas his luxury is not to be mentioned with his munificence, nor is the proscription to find a place on the monument of Augustus.

The best subject for epitaphs is private virtue; virtue exerted in the same circumstances in which the bulk of mankind are placed, and which, therefore, may admit of many imitators. He that has delivered his country from oppression, or freed the world from ignorance and errour, can excite the emulation of a very small number; but he that has repelled the temptations of poverty, and disdained to free himself from distress, at the expense of his virtue, may animate multitudes, by his example, to the same firmness of heart and steadiness of resolution.

Of this kind I cannot forbear the mention of two Greek inscriptions; one upon a man whose writings are well known, the other upon a person whose memory is preserved only in her epitaph, who both lived in slavery, the most calamitous estate in human life:

Ζωσιμη ἡ πριν ἐουσα μονῳ τῳ σωματι δουλη
  Καὶ τῳ σωματι νυν εὑρεν ἐλευθεριην

"Zosima, quæ solo fuit olim corpore serva,
  Corpore nunc etiam libera facta fuit."

"Zosima, who, in her life, could only have her body enslaved, now finds her body, likewise, set at liberty."

It is impossible to read this epitaph without being animated to bear the evils of life with constancy, and to support the dignity of human nature under the most pressing afflictions, both, by the example of the heroine, whose grave we behold, and the prospect of that state in which, to use the language of the inspired writers, "The poor cease from their labours, and the weary be at rest."

The other is upon Epictetus, the Stoick philosopher:

Δουλος Ἐπικτητος γενομην, και σωμ᾽ ἀναπηρος,
Και πενιην Ἰρος, και φιλος Ἀθανατοις.

"Servus Epictetus, mutilatus corpore, vixi
Pauperieque Irus, curaque prima deum."

"Epictetus, who lies here, was a slave and a cripple,
poor as the beggar in the proverb, and the
favourite of heaven."

In this distich is comprised the noblest panegyrick, and the most important instruction. We may learn from it, that virtue is impracticable in no condition, since Epictetus could recommend himself to the regard of heaven, amidst the temptations of poverty and slavery; slavery, which has always been found so destructive to virtue, that in many languages a slave and a thief are expressed by the same word. And we may be, likewise, admonished by it, not to lay any stress on a man's outward circumstances, in making an estimate of his real value, since Epictetus the beggar, the cripple, and the slave, was the favourite of heaven.

Notes

CHAPTER I

1 H. D. Rawnsley, "Reminiscences of Wordsworth among the Peasantry of Westmoreland", in William Knight (ed.), *Wordsworthiana* (London, 1889) pp. 81–119.
2 Ibid.
3 Ibid.
4 *EY*, p. 364.
5 *The Deserted Village*, ll. 265–8.
6 Roger Lonsdale (ed.), *The Poems of Thomas Gray, William Collins, Oliver Goldsmith* (London, 1969) p. 115.
7 *Poems, Chiefly in the Scottish Dialect* (Kilmarnock, 1786) p. iii.
8 Ibid., p. 199.
9 *LY*, ii, p. 700.
10 *MY*, i, p. 195.
11 *Prose Works*, i, pp. 116–17.
12 Love, and the fantasies of lovers, have afforded an ample theme to poets of all ages. Mr Wordsworth, however, has thought fit to compose a piece, illustrating this copious subject by one single thought. A lover trots away to see his mistress one fine evening, gazing all the way on the moon; when he comes to her door,

> O mercy! to myself I cried,
> If Lucy should be dead. (*Edinburgh Review*, April 1808)

13 *Biographia Literaria*, ch. 4.
14 *EY*, p. 264.
15 *Prose Works*, i, pp. 124, 118.
16 *Biographia Literaria*, ch. 17.
17 *Prose Works*, i, p. 128.
18 *Rasselas*, chs 10, 11.
19 John Wilson (1785–1854) later took the pen-name "Christopher North" and became famous for his reviews in *Blackwood's Magazine*. At the time of this correspondence he was an undergraduate at Glasgow University, where he became Professor of Moral Philosophy in 1820.
20 *Prose Works*, iii, pp. 124–5.
21 See Mary Moorman, *William Wordsworth, The Later Years* (Oxford, 1965) p. 100n.

22 *MY,* i, pp. 145–51.
23 For an interesting discussion of these lines see John F. Danby, *The Simple Wordsworth* (London, 1960) pp. 44–5.
24 *MY,* i, pp. 194–6.
25 Ibid., p. 236.
26 Ibid., p. 264.
27 *LY,* ii, p. 664.
28 *PW,* ii, p. 122.
29 *Adventurer,* No. 13.
30 *Biographia Literaria,* ch. 14.
31 *Prose Works,* iii, p. 67ff.
32 Ibid., p. 80.
33 Johnson, *Life of Gray.*
34 Edith J. Morley (ed.), *Henry Crabb Robinson on Books and their Writers* (London, 1938) p. 73.
35 *MY,* ii, p. 190.
36 The quoted items in this paragraph are taken from: *LY,* i, p. 480; *LY,* ii, p. 936; ibid., p. 731; ibid., p. 936; ibid., p. 915.

CHAPTER 2

1 Herbert Lindenberger, *On Wordsworth's "Prelude"* (Princeton, 1963) p. 32.
2 Hugh Blair, *Lectures on Rhetoric,* 3 vols (1811; 1st edn 1783) iii, pp. 311–12.
3 Ibid., pp. 92–3.
4 Ibid., ii, pp. 165–6.
5 *The Prelude,* 1850, viii, ll. 466–7.
6 Alexander B. Grosart, *The Prose Works of William Wordsworth,* 3 vols (London, 1876) iii, p. 426.
7 *PW,* iv, p. 413.
8 *PW,* iii, p. 76.
9 *Prose Works,* ii, pp. 49, 59, 60, 92, 89.
10 *MY,* ii, pp. 179, 196, 301; *LY,* i, pp. 49, 199.
11 *PW,* iii, p. 490.
12 Helen Darbishire, *The Poet Wordsworth* (Oxford, 1950) p. 35.
13 Donald Wesling, *Wordsworth and the Adequacy of Landscape* (London, 1970) p. 47.
14 Mary Jacobus, *Tradition and Experiment in Wordsworth's "Lyrical Ballads"* (Oxford, 1976) p. 9.
15 Op. cit., p. 52.
16 *The Dunciad,* i, ll. 121ff; iv, ll. 53–4.
17 *Prose Works,* ii, p. 66.
18 Johnson, *Life of Pope.*
19 *Prose Works,* ii, pp. 66–9.
20 Ibid., pp. 70–2.
21 Ibid., p. 76.
22 Ibid., p. 83.
23 Ibid., pp. 77, 98.

24 J. W. Mackail, *Select Epigrams from the Greek Anthology* (London, 1906).
25 Ibid., p. 71.
26 Ibid., p. 12.
27 *PW*, ii, pp. 1–13.
28 Salvesen, op. cit., p. 144.
29 Jacobus, op. cit., p. 133.
30 F. W. Bateson, *Wordsworth: A Reinterpretation* (London, 1954) p. 14.
31 *PW*, ii, p. 513.
32 Roger Sharrock, "Wordsworth's Revolt against Literature", in *Wordsworth's Mind and Art*, op. cit., p. 66.
33 Danby, op. cit., p. 44.
34 *Prose Works*, i, p. 133.
35 *LY*, i, p. 437.

CHAPTER 3

1   Op. cit.
2   *Rasselas*, ch. 10.
3   *Idler*, No. 51; *Rambler*, No. 60; *Rambler*, No. 151.
4   Joshua Reynolds, *Fifteen Discourses Delivered in the Royal Academy*, "Discourse VII" (1776). All further quotations from Reynolds in this chapter come from this Discourse unless otherwise stated.
5   Preface to *The Plays of William Shakespeare* (1765).
6   Reynolds, op. cit.
7   Johnson, op. cit.
8   Johnson, *Life of Cowley*.
9   *Prose Works*, iii, p. 80.
10 *Adventurer*, No. 131.
11 *Prose Works*, i, pp. 122–3.
12 Johnson, *Life of Cowley*.
13 *Prose Works*, i, pp. 126–8.
14 Ibid., i, p. 152.
15 *EY*, p. 358.
16 *Prose Works*, i, p. 138.
17 Ibid., i, p. 142.
18 *Prose Works*, ii, p. 57.
19 Herbert Lindenberger, op. cit., pp. 25, 26.
20 *Prose Works*, ii, pp. 56, 59.
21 Ibid., ii, pp. 80, 79, 77.
22 Ibid., ii, p. 57.
23 Appendix, p. 135.
24 *Prose Works*, ii, pp. 58–9.
25 *Biographia Literaria*, ch. 4.
26 *Prose Works*, ii, p. 89; Appendix, p. 130.
27 John Weever, *Ancient Funerall Monuments within the United Monarchie of Great Britaine, Ireland and the Islands adiacent . . . Whereunto is prefixed a Discourse of*

Funerall Monuments . . . Composed by the Studie and Travels of John Weever . . . London . . . *1631*.

CHAPTER 4

1   Op. cit., ch. 4.
2   Ibid., ch. 14.
3   J. K. Stephen, "A Sonnet".
4   Op. cit., pp. 13, 14.
5   Op. cit., ch. 22.
6. Ibid., ch. 14.
7   *Prose Works*, ii, pp. 56, 57, 60.
8   *The Prelude*, 1850, xi, p. 353.
9   *PW*, iv, p. 403.
10 *Prose Works*, iii, p. 33.
11 C. C. Clarke, *Romantic Paradox* (London, 1962) p. 8.
12 *Prose Works*, ii, p. 57.
13 Ibid., p. 58.
14 Ibid., p. 81.
15 Ibid., p. 83.
16 Ibid., p. 68.
17 *Table Talk*, 23 June 1834.
18 *Prose Works*, ii, p. 63.
19 Christopher Salvesen, *The Landscape of Memory* (London, 1905) p. 169.
20 A. de Vere, "Recollections of Wordsworth" (*Essays Chiefly on Poetry*, 1887, ii, pp. 276–7). Quoted by Bateson, op. cit., p. 164.
21 *Prose Works*, ii, p. 84.
22 Ibid., p. 70.
23 Ibid.
24 Ibid., p. 59.
25 Ibid., p. 92.
26 Ibid., p. 85.
27 Ibid, p. 84.
28 Ibid., i, p. 138.
29 Wordsworth was not unsympathetic to puns, even in something so serious as an epitaph. In the second *Essay* he comments on an epitaph in which the writer puns on the name of the dead person:

> It is well known how fond our Ancestors were of a play upon the Name of the Deceased when it admitted of a double sense . . . It brings home a general truth to the individual by the medium of a Pun, which will be readily pardoned, for the sake of the image suggested by it. [*Prose Works*, ii, pp. 67–8].

30 *Prose Works*, ii, pp. 59–60.
31 Ibid., iii, p. 64.

32 Donald Davie, "Dionysus in *Lyrical Ballads*", in A. W. Thomson (ed.), *Wordsworth's Mind and Art* (Edinburgh, 1969) p. 111.
33 *PW*, iv, p. 464.
34 *Prose Works*, ii, p. 17.
35 *PW*, iii, p. 422.
36 Ibid., ii, pp. 506–7.
37 Ibid., p. 472.
38 Ibid., iii, pp. 444–5.
39 Ibid., ii, pp. 50, 53
40 S. M. Parrish, *The Art of "Lyrical Ballads"* (Cambridge, Mass., 1973) p. 14.
41 *PW*, ii, p. 512.

Index